GOLF BALL COVER STORY

Golf Ball Cover Story

What Every Golfer Should Know

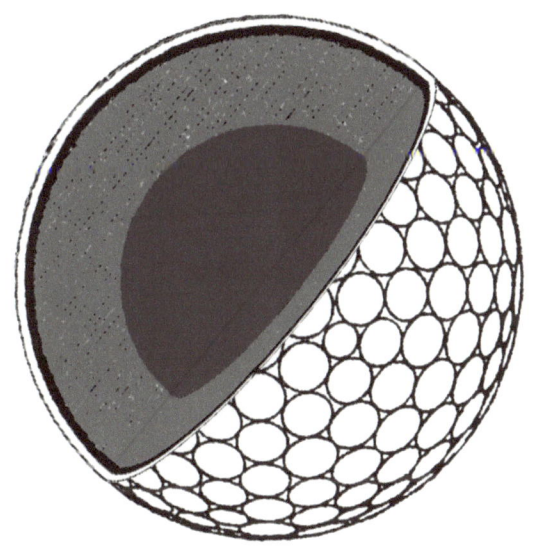

James J. Harrison, PhD

Copyright ©2019 by James J. Harrison
www.golfballcoverstory.com

All rights reserved. This book or any portion thereof may not be reproduced or used in any manner whatsoever without the express written permission of the publisher except for the use of brief quotations in articles and book reviews.

Printed in the United States of America

First Printing, 2018

ISBN-13:978-1939116338 print edition
ISBN-13:978-(your ISBN) ebook edition

Waterside Press
2055 Oxford Ave
Cardiff, CA 92007
www.waterside.com

For Laura

Forward

The reason I started writing this book began innocently enough. I had begun collecting some older Titleist® golf balls. I wanted to know when the golf balls were made and what kind of technology was used to make them. I only found a couple of books that addressed these subjects. After reading them, I realized there were inconsistencies, omissions, and inaccurate information about golf ball dates of introduction and about golf ball technology.

This book is about how the science and technology of golf balls made by Acushnet Company, the maker of Titleist and Pinnacle® golf balls, have advanced from the 1930s to the present. The initial focus is the dimple pattern on the surface of the golf ball. The dimple arrangement and the number of dimples on the golf ball are just about the only thing about a golf ball that can be determined by visual inspection. In order to learn about how and why the dimple patterns on golf balls changed, I started reading the U.S. patent literature from Acushnet Company to find the answer. I soon realized that in addition to changes in the dimple patterns, significant changes were also happening to the materials of construction and the design of the core and the cover of the golf ball. This topic became the second focus of this book. As far as I know, no one has ever written a book that summarizes what the original U.S. patent literature teaches about golf ball science and technology.

This book is important because as a general rule, many golfers don't understand enough about golf ball technology in order to choose which ball they should be playing. Before the 1970s, there were wound golf balls with liquid or solid centers and a balata cover with 336 dimples. Golf balls came in three different compressions: 80 for golfers with slow swing speed, 90 for average swing speeds, and 100 for high swing speeds. That's all there was to it. Today it is much more complicated. This book will explain all the new features of the modern golf ball which will help recreational and professional golfers choose which golf ball they should be using.

This book is also useful because, in general, the date of introduction of Titleist and Pinnacle golf balls into the marketplace has been somewhat difficult to determine. Collectors of Titleist and Pinnacle golf balls may now be able to better determine an accurate date of introduction of these golf balls by knowing the priority date on the U.S. patent that discloses the dimple pattern used on the golf ball.

Although the information contained in the U.S. patent literature may be highly technical in nature and may be written in the specialized language of the legal profession, my background in science and technology and my extensive experience in reading and writing U.S. patents enables me to write in a form and style that is directed to the average reader. Diagrams of the dimple patterns on the surface of the golf ball are especially beautiful from an artistic point of view, and these are used throughout the book.

The first part of this book is organized and arranged using the specific dimple pattern that is being discussed in each chapter. Photographs of the golf balls in my golf ball collection that have that specific dimple pattern are presented throughout the early chapters of the book.

The second part of this book discusses the technology of the Titleist and Pinnacle golf ball models that have different names on the seam such as Pro V1, Pro V1x, NXT Tour, NXT Tour Soft, and so on. This technology was not obtained by visual inspection of the golf balls but rather by reading the U.S. patent literature which is readily available from the covers of the boxes for older Titleist golf balls, or more recently, from the Titleist web page. The U.S. patents describe the science and technology of the cores and the covers of these golf balls and teach what factors are responsible for improved golf ball flight. The reader will also be introduced to the United States Golf Association (USGA) conforming golf ball list, which is an important resource for the golf ball collector and for the recreational and professional golfer. The current USGA conforming golf ball lists have important information that can help golfers decide which golf ball they should be using. The archived USGA conforming golf balls lists, as well as the priority date on the U.S. patents can be useful to the golf ball collector to help pinpoint the date of introduction for a particular model of golf ball.

The book concludes with a chapter that summarizes what I have learned about important golf ball technology. I will answer important questions such as: why does a golf ball feel hard or soft, what causes a golf ball to have high or low spin, what factors will result in a high or low trajectory flight, and what causes one ball to travel farther than another. I also list a set of decision criteria that may help golfers with their golf ball choices.

I have restricted my discussion in this book to golf ball technology that has been patented by Acushnet Company. This is because Acushnet Company is considered by many as the industry leader in golf balls and has been very active in obtaining U.S. patent protection. However, there are many other companies that manufacture and sell golf balls, and these companies apply many of the same scientific principles to the golf balls that they produce.

Table of Contents

Introduction · xi

Chapter One—ATTI Dimple Pattern · 1
Chapter Two—Original Icosahedron Dimple Pattern · · · · · · · · · · 13
Chapter Three—Icosahedron with Dimples of Two Sizes · · · · · · · 31
Chapter Four—Octahedral Dimple Patterns · · · · · · · · · · · · · · · · ·45
Chapter Five—Dimples of Multiple Sizes · · · · · · · · · · · · · · · · · · · 57
Chapter Six—Dimple Patterns for High Swing Speeds · · · · · · · · · 73
Chapter Seven—Symmetric Dimple Patterns · · · · · · · · · · · · · · · · ·81
Chapter Eight—Reduced Distance Golf Balls · · · · · · · · · · · · · · · ·94
Chapter Nine—Low Swing Speeds· 100
Chapter Ten—USGA Conforming Golf Ball List · · · · · · · · · · · · · 105
Chapter Eleven—Titleist Pro V1 Golf Balls · · · · · · · · · · · · · · · · · 108
Chapter Twelve—Titleist Pro V1x Golf Balls · · · · · · · · · · · · · · · · 114
Chapter Thirteen—Titleist NXT, AVX, Tour Soft Golf Balls · · · · · 119
Chapter Fourteen—Titleist Tour, Velocity Golf Balls· · · · · · · · · · 125
Chapter Fifteen—Titleist DT Golf Balls · 129
Chapter Sixteen—Pinnacle Golf Balls · 132
Chapter Seventeen—Vintage Golf Balls ·138
Chapter Eighteen—Summary and Conclusions · · · · · · · · · · · · · · 143

Glossary · 151
Endnotes ·153
Acknowledgements · 161

Introduction

I decided to start a golf ball collection in the fall of 2015 when my wife Laura and I were staying at a bed and breakfast in Pacific Grove California. We would go to Pacific Grove from time to time to enjoy the California coast and get away for a while from the daily routine. While we were there, we got in our car and drove on the 17-Mile Drive to the Pebble Beach Golf Course. We sat in the lodge and ordered a glass of wine and said "hello" to the famous pine tree located near the green on the 18th hole that runs along the edge of Stillwater Cove on the Pacific Ocean.

On one occasion, I stopped at a golf memorabilia shop located near the putting green across from the Pebble Beach Lodge. While I stood looking at the old golf clubs and other memorabilia, I noticed some old mesh golf balls for sale that had square dimples. I remembered I had a golf ball at home with square dimples in my old golf bag. The price tag on the square dimpled ball from the 1920s in the shop was $250. I decided that when I got home, I would find my old golf bag and see if the golf ball was still there. It was!

Figure 1 First golf ball in my golf ball collection.

This ball had U.S. Royal Special 2 on one pole, U.S. Royal Electronic 2 on the other pole, and Cadwell Cover on the seam. I think I found this ball on a golf course that I was playing many years ago. This ball is called a mesh golf ball. It was popular from about 1912 until the 1930s when the golf ball with dimples became more popular. "Cadwell Cover" on the seam refers to a U.S. patent granted in 1934 to Sidney M. Cadwell for curing the balata cover over a wound core. However, this ball seems to be in too good condition for a ball from the 1930s. Hotchkiss[1] reported that during the 1950s U.S. Rubber Company tried to revive the mesh ball and introduced a ball called the "Royal Special". U.S. patent 2,728,5762 issued Dec. 27, 1955 describes a modified mesh ball, which seems to be the same as the ball shown above. I believe this is the ball in my collection and not one from the 1920-1930s.

I can still remember the first time I hit a golf ball. I was 10 years old, and I had gone with my dad to the golf course to watch him play golf. He played while I rode in the golf cart. My dad wasn't a low handicap golfer, but he enjoyed playing, and he played until he was in his early eighties. We were at the Meriden Municipal Golf Course on Westfield Road in Meriden Connecticut, where I grew up. We started on the front nine, and, after the par-3 fourth hole, we were the farthest distance from the club house. So on the fifth tee, my dad asked me if I wanted to hit a golf ball. I said OK and teed up the ball and took a practice swing like I had seen my dad swing. The fifth hole was a par-4 dogleg left, and, after the dogleg, the fairway went downhill to the green. I remember swinging the club and hitting the ball, but I never saw where it went. I asked my dad where it went and he said "It went pretty good down the fairway." I don't remember what happened after that, but I from that time on, I was hooked.

After that, I started playing golf at the Meriden Municipal Golf Course, where it cost only thirty-five cents for nine holes. I remember telling my dad that I shot a score of 70 for nine holes—two shots for a penny. It was the early 1960s. My dad let me use his golf clubs, and I would use the golf balls that he had in his golf bag. In the 1930s my dad had bought a new set of golf clubs which consisted of a matched set of Spalding Autograph AP 40 Robert T. Jones woods that included; a driver, a 2-wood, and a 3-wood with steel shafts, a set of chromium plated "Bristol" Captain matched irons; a 2-mid iron, a 5-mashie, and a 7-mashie niblic with steel shafts, and a putter. I still have the woods and the irons but the putter has been lost. I can remember using golf balls called Acushnet Club Special, Titleist, and Top-Flite. From time to time, I would find golf balls on the golf course and start to use them. All of the golf balls available at that time would form a cut on the cover if you didn't hit them properly. Since I was just learning how to hit the ball properly, that would happen quite frequently. I would still play with a golf ball with a small cut in it, but if it had more than one cut, or if it had a big, deep cut I would throw it away or hit it into the woods.

My dad worked as a press photographer at the local newspaper, the Meriden Record Journal. This turned out to be fortunate because at one point, the Spalding Autograph AP 40 Robert T. Jones driver needed to be repaired. It seems that the driver, the 2-wood, and the 3-wood all had lead weights at the bottom of the clubs, presumably because more weight at the bottom of the clubs resulted in improved performance. One day the lead weight on the driver broke, and the piece of lead fell out of the club, leaving a gap in the back of the driver. My dad and I went to the newspaper building where he worked, carrying the broken driver. We went into a room where they had a cauldron of liquid lead that was used in some way to create the letters used in the printing of the newspaper. After my dad explained what had happened to the driver, the workers happily rigged up a stand to hold the golf club. Then they poured a small amount of lead into the gap in the driver. The fix wasn't perfect but it was sufficient to let us continue to use the driver.

When I was fourteen, I heard about the Meriden City golf championship, and I decided to enter. By then I was shooting in the 90s and sometimes in the high 80s for 18 holes. I was still playing with my father's golf clubs. The players were arranged in 6 flights arranged according to ability. I was entered in the lowest flight. The format was match play, and I played grown men much older than I was at the time. I won my first match, then my second match, and my third match. In the fourth match I was playing in the semi-finals against a player who was about 35 years old. He was a pretty good golfer, and I found myself two holes down after 16 holes. On the 17th hole, a par three, I scored a par and he scored a bogey, so I was one hole down with one left to play. The 18th hole was a par four, about 280 yards down a big hill, out of bounds on the right, with the green located on top of a small rise. We both hit good drives down to the bottom of the hill. My opponent was away and hit first. His shot went right on the green and, although I couldn't see exactly where he ended up, I thought he was close to the pin. I hit next, and my shot was also right on the green, close to the pin, although I couldn't see exactly how close. When I got to the green I found that my opponent's ball was about 5-feet away from the cup. My ball was in the cup for an eagle two! My opponent sank his putt for a birdie, but we were now tied and had to go to extra holes. On the first extra hole, I shot a six and my opponent shot a seven resulting in me being the winner. Right then I realized I loved the sport of golf, and hoped I could play this game forever.

In the finals I played a boy, who was a year younger than me and a very good golfer. I think his entire family was into golf—his father played and he had a sister who also played golf. I played probably the best golf I had ever played during our match. Our match was nip and tuck, with my opponent sometimes one up, and sometimes I was one up. I found myself on the 18th tee, one hole down. It was now do or die. On the 18th hole we both hit good drives to the bottom of the hill and I hit first. My shot went onto the green ending up about ten feet away. My opponent's shot went onto the green and ended up about eight feet away. I knew I had to sink my putt and he had to miss his so that we could go to a sudden death playoff. I lined up my putt and sank it. My opponent then calmly walked up to his putt, lined it up and sank it for the win.

The awards ceremony took place later behind the 18th green when the players in the 1st flight finished playing their final match. It was a happy occasion for me, because I never in my wildest dreams thought I had a chance in the Meriden City Championship. Here is a copy of a photo that was taken during the awards ceremony as I stepped up to claim my second place prize—a sleeve of golf balls. The golf professional, George Hunter, is in the foreground with his back to the camera. The Meriden Municipal Golf Course is now named George Hunter Municipal Golf Course in his honor.

Figure 2 Awards ceremony at the Meriden City Championship[3]

So, getting back to my golf ball collection, what started as a serendipity observation of a golf ball with square dimples in a golf shop at Pebble Beach, has evolved into an interesting and fun discovery of the joys of a golf ball collection and the technology that is important in constructing golf balls. In the pages that follow, I summarize what I have learned about golf ball technology from sources that were readily available to me. First, were the dimple patterns on the ball. Anyone can easily determine by inspection the number of dimples and the arrangement of dimples on the ball. Second was the published U.S. patent literature.

The golf balls in my collection were obtained originally from my dad's old golf bag that I kept in the garage for many years. The second source is from E-BAY, the on-line site where you can purchase golf balls that are offered for sale from time to time. The third source is friends who have located golf balls in old golf bags or odd places in their homes, and have offered them to me to include in my golf ball collection.

Chapter One
ATTI Dimple Pattern (336 A)

The ATTI dimple pattern on a golf ball consists of 336 dimples arranged in an octahedral pattern with 42 dimples in eight sections. The ball has a seam or parting line at the equator and there are 168 dimples on each side of the equator. The dimples are evenly distributed about the surface of the golf ball. This dimple pattern was named after Raphael Atti.[1] He produced most of the dimple pattern molds for the whole golf ball industry in the early 1900s. Virtually all dimpled golf balls were made with the ATTI pattern until the 1970s. I call this the 336 A dimple pattern.

Dimples on golf balls first appeared in 1908 when William Taylor[2] obtained a patent for a golf ball whose object was to obtain better results in the flight of the golf ball. The patent taught that "better results can be obtained by using isolated cavities (dimples), circular in plan and evenly distributed on the surface of the ball. The cavities must be shallow, and circular, with steep sides at the edges, and a depth not exceeding one eighth of the diameter of the cavity. The diameter of the cavity must not be less than 0.09 nor greater than 0.15 inch, and the depth must not exceed 0.014 inch. Preferably the cavities should occupy not less than a quarter or more than three quarters of the entire surface of the ball." The dimples on the surface of a golf ball quickly replaced brambles (bumps) on the ball and competed with the mesh pattern, which dimples eventually replaced in the 1930s.

Why were 336 dimples chosen for the ATTI dimple pattern? To find out, I looked at the specifications in the Taylor dimple patent to see if that could give me any clues. The patent teaches that the diameter of the cavities must not be less than 0.09 or greater than 0.15 inch. Preferably the cavities should occupy not less than a quarter (25%) or more than three quarters (75%) of the entire surface of the ball. The patent doesn't teach us what the diameter of the ball was, but assuming that the diameter was about 1.60 inch (the diameter of the golf ball was set to 1.62 inches in 1921),[3] then I could calculate the percent coverage for a ball with 336 dimples as a function of the dimple diameter as shown in Figure 1.1. This shows me that a ball with 336 dimples will cover about 27% of the surface when the dimple diameter is 0.09 inch and will cover about 74% of the surface when the dimple diameter is 0.15 inch. This fact, plus the fact that the number 336 is evenly divided by eight, probably was a factor in the development of the octahedral dimple pattern in the Taylor patent.

Ball Diameter In.	Ball Surface Area sq. in.	Dimple Diameter in.	No. of Dimples	Dimple Area sq. In.	% surface coverage
1.60	8.04	0.09	336	2.14	27
1.60	8.04	0.12	336	3.80	47
1.60	8.04	0.15	336	5.94	74

Figure 1.1 Calculation of percent coverage, dimple diameter and number of dimples for Taylor patent

In 1899, Bertram G. Work and Coburn Haskell[4] obtained a patent for a wound golf ball that was light and durable, non-resilient under moderate impacts, and highly resilient under strong impacts. This ball had a central core of gutta-percha that was wound with a rubber thread under tension into spherical form and then covered with a shell of gutta-percha or balata gum. The cover consisted of a series of raised bumps called brambles which was the state of the art at that time. Later the cover consisted of dimples. The wound ball continued to be produced in various forms until the late 1990s.

The first wound balls were made by hand. This proved to be difficult to do, because the rubber thread was pulled tight with one hand while the other hand held and rotated the ball. In 1900, John R. Gammeter obtained a patent[5] for a machine that would wind the thread around the golf ball. One drawback to the Gammeter ball winding machine was it operated to maintain a constant pull on the thread being wound on the ball. Since the rubber thread sometimes is not uniform in width, when the width is too small, the rubber is stretched to a greater degree and when the width is too wide, the rubber is stretched to a lesser degree. The result was a golf ball that had a variation in the winding density. In 1947, Kurt E. Wilhelm obtained a patent[6] that provided a high degree of uniformity in the winding density. This was accomplished by applying the thread to the golf ball under constant winding tension (tensile stress) and not under constant pull (tensile force).

In 1908, Frank H. Mingay[7] obtained a patent for a golf ball that contained an incompressible liquid, such as water in a rubber pouch, as a central core that was further wound with a rubber thread under tension and then covered. This became known as a liquid center wound golf ball.

Gutta-percha[8] (balata) is a polymer of isoprene which was first obtained in 1842 from the sap of a tree that grows in Malaysia. The milk sap from the tree is called latex which consists of about 60% water, 28% solid rubber particles suspended in an emulsion, resins, proteins, and sugars dissolved in the water. Gutta-percha (balata) is a thermoplastic material. This means that it is a pliable polymer that can be molded when heated and solidifies upon cooling. This enabled a cover to be molded on the surface of a golf ball by placing a sheet of gutta-percha (balata) over the core of the golf ball and heating the surface of the ball with the mold which contained the desired dimple pattern. The advantage of this was that the gutta-percha (balata) was relatively strong and was able to protect the rubber winding around the core from unraveling. The disadvantage was that during a warm day the gutta-percha (balata) could soften and the golf ball could lose its shape. The problem of the gutta-percha (balata) cover softening and losing its shape on hot days was solved in 1925 when William C. Geer[9] patented a golf ball with a vulcanized balata cover.

The Geer patent used an accelerator to promote rapid vulcanization of the balata cover. The Geer process consisted of mixing together balata, zinc oxide, and sulfur in one batch and then mixing an accelerator and raw rubber in a second batch. These two batches were then milled together, rolled into sheets and then the sheet was cut into circular pieces in the desired shape to form the top and bottom halves of the golf ball cover. The two circular pieces were pressed on opposite sides of the golf ball core and then the ball and cover was placed in the mold to fuse the two halves of the cover together and to form the desired dimple pattern on the surface of the ball. This took place at elevated pressure and temperature, but care had to be taken so that the rubber windings around the core were not over-heated.

The wound core of the golf ball was prepared using a special machine that automatically wound rubber thread around the core of the golf ball.

Figure 1.2 Machine that was used for winding the rubber thread around a golf ball[10]

The sheets of balata were cut into circles and then pressed into the desired shape to form the top and bottom halves of the cover of the golf ball.

Figure 1.3 Top and bottom halves of the cover before being pressed over the core[10]

The wound core of the golf ball was covered with the top and bottom halves of the balata cover and then heated in a mold to vulcanize the cover on the golf ball. Of course the excess material at the seam of the ball still had to be removed. This excess material had to be discarded because vulcanization had already occurred.

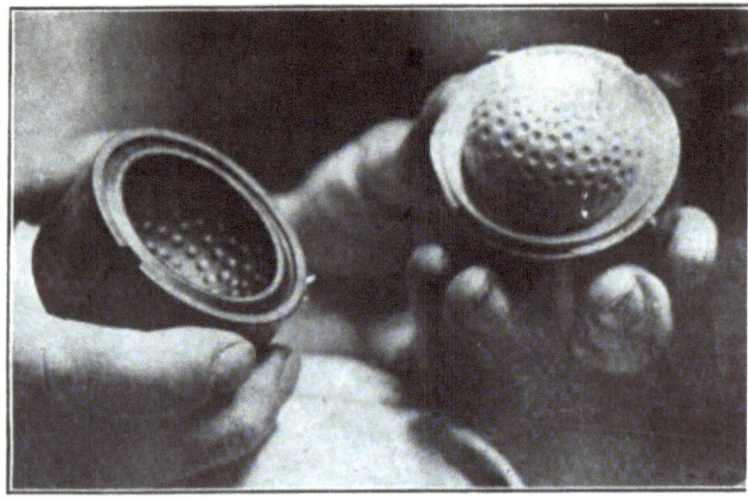

Figure 1.4 Golf ball still in the mold after vulcanization[10]

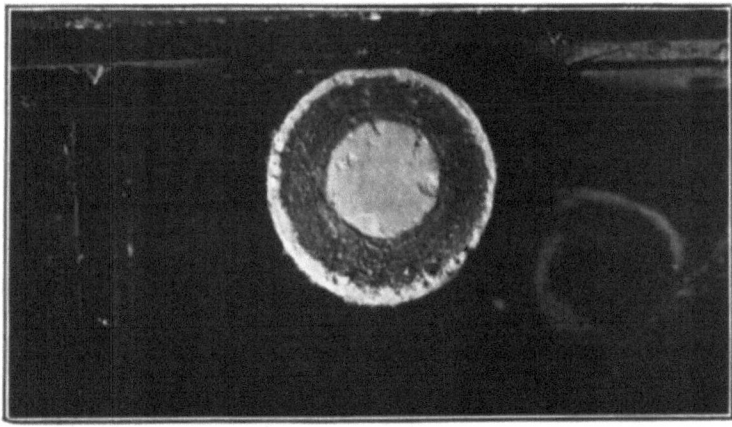

Figure 1.5 A golf ball cut in half with the core, rubber windings, and cover[10]

The problem of over-heating of the rubber windings around the core of the golf ball with the Geer process was solved in 1934 when Sidney M. Cadwell[11] obtained a patent for an improved vulcanization process. In this patent, balata, zinc sulfide, zinc oxide, sulfur, and dibenzylamine were first combined to form a stock composition that was milled and stored until needed without fear of set-up or vulcanization during storage. Then the cover stock was made into sheets, cut into circular pieces, pressed onto the golf ball core, and molded at lower temperature so that the rubber windings were not damaged. After removing the dimpled ball from the mold, the excess material at the seam was cut off and recombined with the unused cover stock for use later. This became very attractive for golf ball manufacturers because it reduced the overall cost. Then vulcanization was started by adding a dilute emulsion of carbon disulfide and the golf ball was heated. The carbon disulfide reacted with the dibenzylamine to form a powerful vulcanizing agent. The golf balls were then washed and dried.

The two patents obtained by Geer and Cadwell essentially solved the problems of the gutta-percha balls losing their shape in hot weather and overheating the rubber windings in the core during vulcanization of the cover. It has been reported that all golf ball manufacturers took out licenses from the two patents to practice this technology.[12] Another reference reported that the Geer and Cadwell patents were merged.[13] But this is less likely because usually, only patent applications from the same company are merged. Assigning dates of production for antique golf balls from this period can be made with this information. As a general rule, golf balls that had 'Geer Patent Cover' on the seam of the ball were probably made after the Geer patent issued (1925) but before the Cadwell patent issued (1934). Golf balls that had 'Cadwell Geer Cover' or simply 'Cadwell Geer' on the seam of the ball probably were produced after 1934, when all golf ball manufacturers had taken out licenses.

The Acushnet Process Company was formed in 1910 by Philip E. Young[14] and began supplying latex and rubber to industry. In 1932, the company was divided into two divisions, Rubber and Golf, and it took three years to perfect the first Titleist golf ball. The story goes that Philip E. Young was playing golf and realized that the ball he was using was not producing uniform spin and movement. He asked his dentist to take an x-ray of the ball and found that the center core of the ball was misaligned. Young teamed up with his friend Fred Bommer and made improvements in the process of making golf balls. Using the best golf ball technology of the day obtained from the patents discussed above, Acushnet was able in 1935 to produce a liquid center wound ball with a balata cover that produced the desired spin and movement. They first froze the liquid core of the golf ball before winding it with rubber winding, so the core would be perfectly aligned in the center of the ball.

Figure 1.6 The *Titleist Professional 3, Acushnet, Geer Patent Cover* golf ball #69[15] is one of the earliest golf balls made by the Acushnet Company that I have in my golf ball collection.

Ball #69 (Figure 1.6) has 'Titleist Professional 3' on the two poles of the ball, 'Acushnet' on one seam, and 'Geer Patent Cover' on the other seam. The ball has the ATTI dimple pattern with 336 dimples. The ball was wound and had a liquid center. I have dated the production of this ball at 1932-1934 based on the fact that the Golf division of Acushnet Process Company was founded in 1932 and on the fact that the seam label says 'Geer Patent Cover', which means it was produced before the Cadwell patent was allowed (1934). Most of the golf balls from this period of time are yellowed with age and show cracks and other imperfections on the cover.

Figure 1.7 The *Titleist Acushnet 4, Cadwell Geer Cover* golf ball #39 is another early Titleist golf ball in my collection.

Ball #39 (Figure 1.7) has '*Titleist Acushnet 4*' on both poles of the ball and 'Cadwell Geer Cover' on one of the seams. This ball is reported to have been produced around 1943[16] which is consistent with the label 'Cadwell Geer Cover' on the seam. This ball has 336 dimples and is a liquid center wound ball with a balata cover.

Philip Young had asked his dentist to run x-rays on the early Titliest golf balls to make sure the center was consistently round. I was able to obtain dental x-rays on the *Titleist Professional* 3, *Acushnet, Geer Patent Cover* golf ball #69 and the *Titleist Acushnet 4, Cadwell Geer Cover* golf ball #39. These x-rays were obtained by placing the golf balls on the dental x-ray sensor fastened onto a flat surface and then taking the x-ray from above. The dental sensor was smaller in size than the diameter of the golf balls and therefore only part of the golf ball was displayed. The outside edge of the golf ball only appears in the lower right hand corner of the x-ray. The outer surface of the golf ball has been drawn by hand on the x-ray pictures of the golf balls based on the estimated center of the golf ball and the outside edge. The white region in the x-ray is the liquid center of the golf ball, the grey area extending out from the center region is the wound area of the ball, and at the visible edge in the lower right hand corner of the x-ray is the cover of the golf ball.

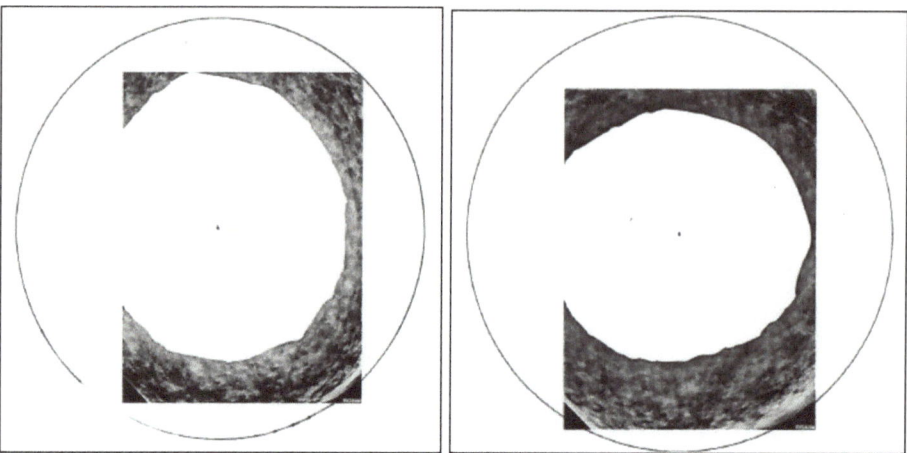

Figure 1.8 Dental x-rays of ball #69 (left) and ball #39 (right).

The x-ray of the *Titleist Professional* 3, *Acushnet, Geer Patent Cover* golf ball #69 (Figure 1.8 left) shows that the liquid center of the golf ball was not quite circular in shape but rather an oval. In contrast, the x-ray of the *Titleist Acushnet 4, Cadwell Geer Cover* golf ball #39 (Figure 1.8 right) was very nearly circular. This supports the idea that the manufacturing process that produced ball #69 had not yet been optimized (before 1935), and the process that produced ball #39 had been optimized and was produced later (after 1935).

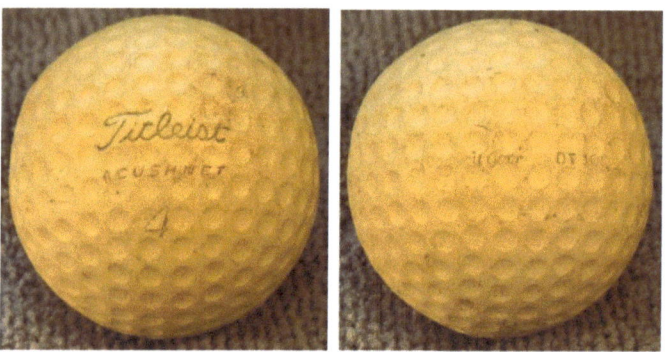

Figure 1.9 *The Titleist Acushnet 4, Cadwell Geer DT 100 golf ball #145*

Ball #145 (Figure 1.9) has '*Titleist Acushnet 4*' on the poles and '*Cadwell Geer* DT 100' on the seam. This ball resembles ball #39 in the pole markings but differs in the marking on the seam. This seam marking has the letters 'Cadwell Geer DT 100'. The DT refers to technology that Acushnet began using in 1947-1949, which is called "dynamite thread" technology.[17] The technology called 'dynamite thread' produced a golf ball that traveled farther than previous golf balls. I think that the Acushnet 'dynamite thread' technology used a variation in the winding technology discussed in reference 6 above. One variation[18] used a winding process that supplied the rubber thread to the golf ball under constant tension, and not under a constant pull as heretofore. This process greatly reduced the variations in the degree of stretch of the rubber thread on the ball and the final density and flight of the golf ball.

Acushnet Company also produced a series of golf balls with 'Acushnet' and (two circles with center dots) on one pole and the 'model name' plus (two circles with center dots) on the other pole. The model names included Bradford, Green Ray, Pinnacle, Finalist, and Titleist. I have two examples of these in my golf ball collection—the Acushnet Titleist and the Acushnet Finalist. Shown below are the photos of the early Acushnet Titleist (Figure 1.10) and the Acushnet Finalist (Figure 1.11).

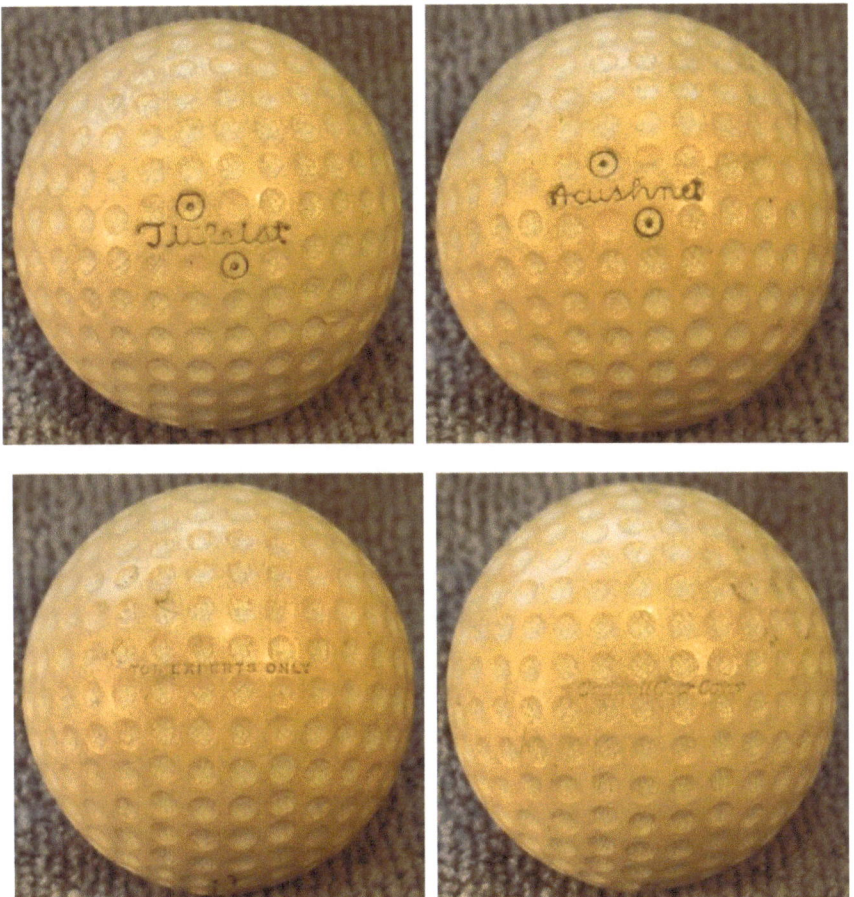

Figure 1.10 The *Acushnet, Titleist, Cadwell Geer Cover,* FOR EXPERTS ONLY, ball #97

Ball #97 (Figure 1.10) was probably produced after the Cadwell patent issued (1934) and before the Geer patent expired (1942), but also before the dynamite thread technology was introduced (1948), because the label on the seam says

'Cadwell Geer Cover' and the DT is missing. The label on the other seam 'FOR EXPERTS ONLY' seems to be rather odd, but may indicate that Acushnet Company was interested in catering to professional golfers and not the average player. This golf ball also looks like it was painted because if you look closely it still has some white paint remaining inside the dimples compared to the golf ball in Figure 1.6.

Figure 1.11 *The Acushnet, Finalist, Cadwell Geer D7 ball #47*

Ball #47 (Figure 1.11) has Acushnet (two circles with center dots) on one pole and has Finalist[19] (two circles with center dots) on the other pole. It was probably produced after the Cadwell patent issued (1934) and before the Geer patent expired (1942) because the label on the seam says Cadwell Geer D7. I don't know what the label 'D7' means. The Finalist model was probably made to appeal to the average golfer rather than the professional.

Figure 1.12 *The Titleist 6, Acushnet DT, Made In U.S.A golf ball #48*

Ball #48 (Figure 1.12) is a wound ball with a liquid center and a balata cover. This ball was made with the dynamite thread technology as evidenced by the DT on the seam of the ball. This ball was probably produced after 1947 but before 1973.

Figure 1.13 *Titleist 6, Acushnet DT Red* golf ball #23

Ball #23 (Figure 1.13) is a wound ball with a liquid center and a balata cover. The dynamite thread technology was used to prepare this ball, which had a lower compression (80 compression) than a ball with a black Titleist logo with a red number (90 compression), or a black Titleist logo with a black number (100 compression). Notice the damage to the balata cover that probably resulted from the ball striking a tree or a paved path or road. This ball was probably introduced in the 1950s.[20]

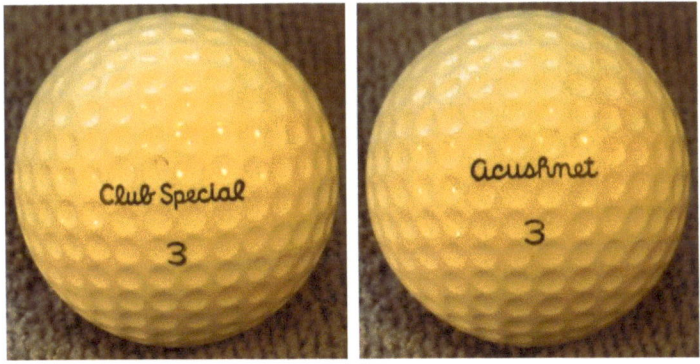

Figure 1.14 *The Acushnet 3, Club Special 3, golf ball #34*

Ball #34 (Figure 1.14) is a wound ball with a liquid center that has 336 dimples arranged in the ATTI pattern. I believe it has a synthetic balata cover (polyisoprene) that was available beginning in the 1980s.

Synopsis Chapter One

- The ATTI dimple pattern contained 336 dimples arranged in an octahedral dimple pattern on the surface of the golf ball (336 A).

- This dimple pattern dominated the golf ball industry from the 1920's to the 1970's.
- During this period of time all golf balls were wound with a liquid or rubber center and had a soft balata cover.
- Geer (1925) and Cadwell (1934) obtained patents for vulcanizing the balata cover on the golf ball.
- Acushnet Company started making golf balls around 1935.
- Acushnet Company developed 'dynamite thread' technology in 1948.

Chapter Two
Original Icosahedron Dimple Pattern (324 IA, 332 IA, 384 IB, 392 IB) Priority Date 1972

The ATTI dimple pattern on a golf ball dominated the golf ball industry from the early 1920s until the 1970s. This pattern consisted of 336 dimples arranged in an octahedron pattern with 42 dimples arranged in eight triangular sections. An octahedron[1] is a geometric figure with eight triangular faces, six vertices and twelve edges. Figure 2.1 shows an orthographic representation of an octahedron on the surface of a sphere.

Figure 2.1 Orthographic representation of an octahedron[1]

In 1973, Acushnet introduced a new Titleist golf ball that abandoned the ATTI dimple pattern. Acushnet developed a new golf ball over a seven-year period of wind tunnel testing and evaluation that resulted in a golf ball that had improved distance. The dimples on this ball were arranged in an icosahedron dimple pattern. An icosahedron[2] is a geometric figure with twenty triangular faces, twelve vertices, and thirty edges. This is shown in Figure 2.2, which is an orthographic representation of an icosahedron on the surface of a sphere.

Figure 2.2 Orthographic representation of an icosahedron[2]

Lynch et al filed patents in Great Britain[3] and in the United States[4-6] in 1972 for this invention. In the United States, a patent is a right granted to the inventor for a process (method), machine, product, or composition of matter that is new, useful, and not obvious. A patent gives the inventor an exclusive right to the technology for a limited time and prevents anyone else to make, use, or sell the invention for 17 years after the patent is allowed. In 1995, the United States Patent and Trademark Office changed the time rule to last for 20 years after the patent is filed. After the patent term expires, the new technology enters the public domain and is free for anyone to use. This is done to encourage inventors to disclose new technology to the world so that technology will be able to continuously improve, and to give the inventor a limited time monopoly on the new technology.

I call this new dimple pattern the 'original icosahedron' pattern (324 IA). The original patents claimed golf balls with 332 and 392 dimples. Figure 2.3 is the dimple patterns looking from the top or polar region of the golf ball that shows the difference in the dimple patterns between the ATTI pattern (left) and the original icosahedron pattern (right).

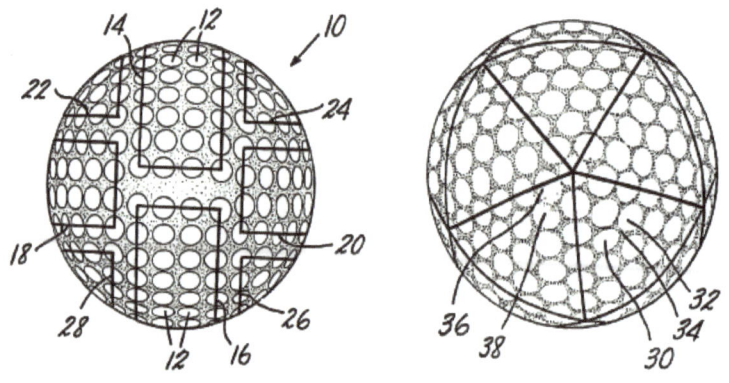

Figure 2.3 Polar view, ATTI pattern (left) and original icosahedron pattern (right)[4]

Clearly the two dimple patterns are different. But, is an icosahedron pattern novel? Isn't an icosahedron one of the original Platonic solids? The five Platonic solids (tetrahedron, cube, octahedron, dodecahedron and icosahedron)[7] have been known since antiquity. Wouldn't it be obvious to one skilled in the art to simply replace one Platonic solid with another? These are the types of questions that a skilled patent examiner would ask the inventor before the patent can be granted. The patent examiner also would most likely ask the inventor to show some test data that shows usefulness—data that proves the golf ball with the icosahedron dimple pattern is better in some way than the golf ball of the prior art. As it turns out, the original Lynch et al patents did not contain any data that showed improved performance. Lynch et al had a long and difficult time convincing the patent examiner that their invention was novel, useful, and not obvious. The original patent application was abandoned, revised, and re-examined many times, then filed again in 1985 and finally was allowed in 1988.

This patent situation resulted in a rather contentious situation in the golf ball industry. Acushnet began producing golf balls with 324 dimples in the original icosahedron dimple pattern and introduced them in the U.S. market in 1973. These golf balls were called Titleist Regular (90 compression) and Titleist 100[8]. But the U.S. patents protecting this technology were not allowed until 1988. The golf ball with 324 dimples in the original icosahedron dimple pattern ended up unprotected in the U.S. until 1988. The British patent had appeared by 1975. This new golf ball was patent protected in Great Britain. So in the U.S., many other golf ball manufacturers who weren't aware of any U.S. Acushnet patents were able to obtain the Titliest golf balls with the new technology. They analyzed the new dimple pattern and manufactured and sold their own copies of the icosahedron dimple technology in the U.S. until 1988. Spalding was one such company. Acushnet and Spalding "spent considerable time in court from 1981 to 1990 hashing out patent issues.[9] The initial dispute involved Spalding's 1974 patent for a sodium and zinc golf ball cover called Surlyn®. Surlyn was a major advance because it prevented excessive cracking on the cover of the golf ball. Acushnet and a number of other ball manufacturers adopted the formula for the Surlyn cover and Spalding went to court to protect its patent. After eight years of litigation, a federal judge in 1989 ruled against Acushnet. Acushnet filed an appeal that sued Spalding over patent violations regarding golf ball dimple patterns, fluorescent ball covering, and golf ball molding. Finally, in November 1990, the two companies settled their differences, agreeing to a cross-licensing of patents.[9]

The dimples in the original icosahedron dimple pattern that are shown in Figure 2.3 were arranged in a number of triangular regions. There was one dimple on each of the vertices of the triangular regions, five dimples on the edges of the triangular regions, and ten dimples inside the triangular regions. You would expect a regular icosahedron which contains 12 vertices, 30 edges, and 20 triangles to contain a total of 362 dimples. Interestingly, the picture of the icosahedron pattern golf ball in Figure

2.3 only showed the polar region of the golf ball. The equatorial region was not shown, because, as we shall see, the original icosahedron pattern was not a regular icosahedron, but rather an icosahedron that was modified in the equatorial region.

The dimples are formed on the surface of the golf ball during the manufacturing process using two molds that contained the desired dimple pattern. At the equator of the golf ball is a seam that is formed by removing the excess cover material when the two molds are removed from the finished ball. In Figure 2.3, there are the two polar regions of the golf ball that contain of a total of 212 dimples. A regular icosahedron, where all triangular regions have five dimples on each edge and ten dimples inside each triangular region, would have a total of 362 dimples; however, this would produce a ball with one row of dimples located at the equator or seam of the golf ball. It is very difficult to remove the excess seam material that is formed in molding the cover of the ball if the seam lies directly on top of one row of dimples. To overcome this problem, Acushnet ended up making two icosahedron dimple patterns—one with 392 dimples and the other with 332 dimples. The ball with 392 dimples contained six rows of thirty dimples in the equatorial region. The ball with 332 dimples contained four rows of thirty dimples in the equatorial region. This resulted in two new dimple patterns where the seam of the golf ball did not lie directly on top of a row of dimples. Figure 2.4 shows an isometric view of the original icosahedron dimple pattern with 392 dimples. The ball with 332 dimples has the same pattern as the one with 392 dimples except that one row of dimples above the equator and one row below the equator are removed.

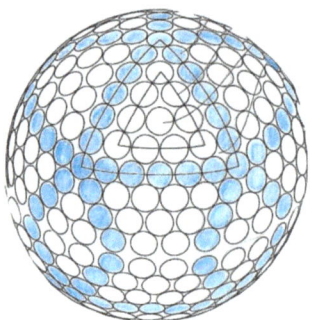

Figure 2.4 An Isometric view of the original icosahedron with 392 dimples

The Titleist golf balls with the original icosahedron dimple pattern that were produced starting in the 1970's had three dimples removed for the Titleist label and one dimple removed for the identifying number on each half of the ball. This resulted in a Titleist golf ball with 324 dimples instead of 332 dimples, and 384 dimples instead of 392 dimples. In the late 1980s Acushnet changed this and stopped removing dimples for the label and number.

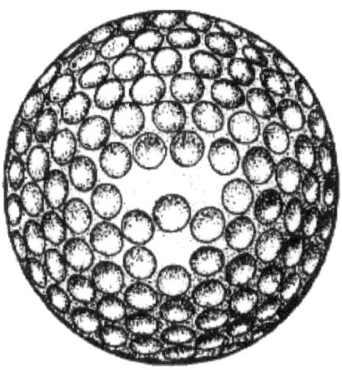

Figure 2.5 Polar view dimple pattern 324 IA with dimples removed[10]

The space between the dimples was an important factor. The ATTI dimple pattern had each dimple surrounded by eight other dimples, as shown in Figure 2.6.

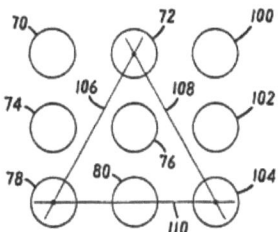

Figure 2.6 ATTI dimple arrangement[4]

In the original icosahedron dimples pattern, each dimple was surrounded by only six dimples, as shown in Figure 2.7. This can be used as a quick and easy way to date early Titleist golf balls. If the golf ball has dimples surrounded by eight other dimples, then it has the ATTI dimple pattern and was produced before 1973. If the golf ball has dimples surrounded by only six other dimples, then it is likely the original icosahedron dimple pattern and was produced after 1973-5.

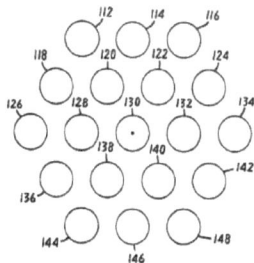

Figure 2.7 Original Icosahedron dimple arrangement[4]

Generally, the only way to differentiate golf balls produced in the 1970-1990s, was by the compression number. The compression number was measured using a compression tester invented by Raphael Atti.[11] The compression number was proportional to a ball's velocity. There were three different golf ball compression numbers in general use—80, 90, and 100. A golf ball with a compression number of 80 (identified by a red name and number) was generally used by a golfer with a slow swing speed, 90 (black name and red number or red name and black number) by a golfer with an average swing speed, and 100 (black name and black number) by a golfer with a very high swing speed. That was all there was to it.

Photographs of Golf Balls with the Original Icosahedron Dimple Pattern
Titleist golf balls with the 324 IA dimple pattern

Figure 2.8 *Titleist 4*, Acushnet golf ball #1 (324 IA)

Ball #1 (Figure 2.8) is a wound ball with a liquid center that has 324 dimples arranged in the original icosahedron dimple pattern (324 IA). This ball was called Titleist Regular, and it was introduced in 1973. It has a balata cover, and the compression is 90. Note the wide space located at the equator of the golf ball that does not contain any dimples. This wide space is called the seam of the ball and it is the place where the excess cover material was removed after vulcanization.

Figure 2.9 *Titleist* 7 Acushnet-Pro Traj ball #2 (324 IA)

Ball #2 (Figure 2.9) is a wound ball with a liquid center that has 324 dimples arranged in the original icosahedron dimple pattern (324 IA). It was introduced in 1975 and had a balata cover. Notice the cracks in the cover of this golf ball due to the soft balata cover.

Figure 2.10 *Titleist* 3 Pro Trajectory 90 ball # 58 (324 IA)

Ball #58 (Figure 2.10) is a wound ball with a liquid center that has 324 dimples arranged in the original icosahedron dimple pattern (324 IA). It has a balata cover, was introduced in 1979, and the compression was 90.

Figure 2.11 *Titleist 7*, Pro Trajectory 100 golf ball #4 (324 IA)

Ball #4 (Figure 2.11) is a wound ball with a liquid center that has 324 dimples arranged in the original icosahedron dimple pattern (324 IA). It was introduced in 1979, had a balata cover, and the compression was 100.

Figure 2.12 DT *Titleist 8*, Durable Titleist 90 ball #7 (324 IA)

Ball #7 (Figure 2.12) is a wound ball with a liquid center that has 324 dimples arranged in the original icosahedron dimple pattern (324 IA). It has a Surlyn cover, was introduced in 1974, and the compression was 90.

Figure 2.13 DT *Titleist 4*, Durable SURLYN golf ball #129 (324 IA)

Ball #129 (Figure 2.13) is also a wound ball with a liquid center that has 324 dimples arranged in the original icosahedron dimple pattern (324 IA). It has a Surlyn cover, was introduced in 1974, and the compression was 90.

Figure 2.14 DT *Titleist 5*, Durable Titleist 90 golf ball #130 (324 IA)

Ball #130 (Figure 2.14) is also a wound ball with a liquid center that has 324 dimples arranged in the original icosahedron dimple pattern (324 IA). It has a Surlyn cover, was introduced in 1974, and the compression was 90.

Figure 2.15 *Titleist 2,* Acushnet DT golf ball #146 (324 IA)

Ball #146 (Figure 2.15) is also a wound ball with a liquid center that has 324 dimples arranged in the original icosahedron dimple pattern (324 IA). The word Titleist on this ball is colored red/brown, which may mean that it is a ball with low compression i.e., 80. Because the seam contains the term Acushnet DT, this ball used the 'dynamite thread' winding technology introduced in 1947, which had not appeared on the other original icosahedron dimple pattern golf balls.

Pinnacle Golf Ball with 324 IA Dimple Pattern

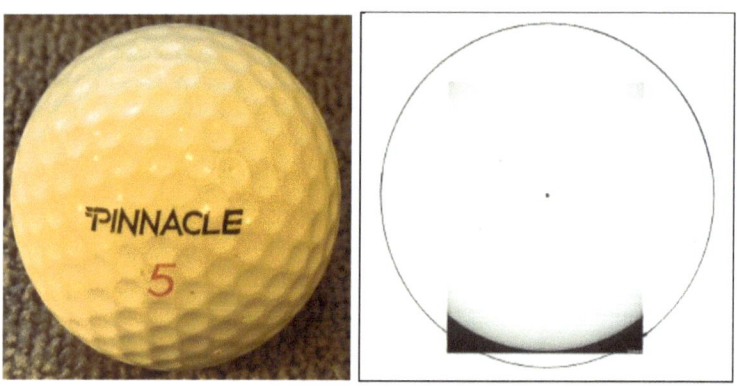

Figure 2.16 Pinnacle 5 golf ball #13 (324 IA, left) and partial x-ray image (right)

Ball #13 (Figure 2.16) is a two-piece golf ball with 324 dimples arranged in the original icosahedron dimple pattern (324 IA) and a balata cover. The two-piece core was made from polybutadiene crosslinked with an unsaturated carboxylic acid and a free radical initiator.[12] At first, I wasn't sure if this ball was a wound ball with a solid core or a two-piece ball. In order to find out, I obtained a dental x-ray for this ball. The detector for the x-ray was smaller than the size of the golf ball so only a partial image of the ball could be seen. I have located the center of the golf ball using Thales theorem[13] and have drawn a circle (1.68 inch diameter) where the cover would be located had the entire ball been observed. The x-ray conclusively showed that this ball was a two-piece ball. As best as I can tell, this ball was introduced in 1982 and was called the Pinnacle 2-piece.

Pinnacle Golf Balls with 332 IA Dimple Pattern

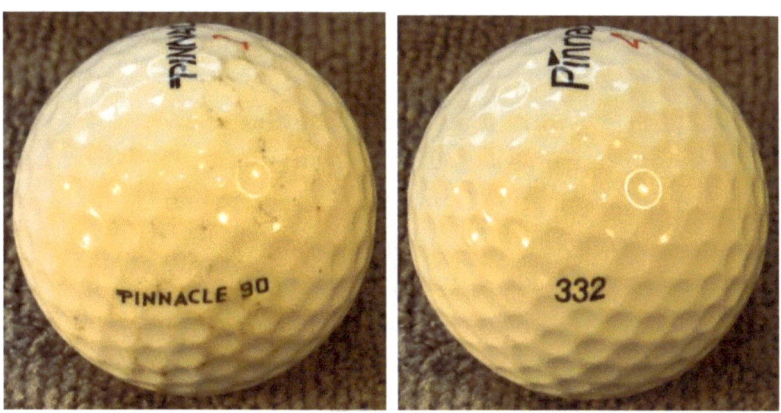

Figure 2.17 Pinnacle golf balls #99 (332 IA, left) and #33 (332 IA, right)

These two Pinnacle golf balls (Figure 2.17) have the original icosahedron dimple pattern (332 IA) where eight dimples were not removed for the name and the number.

In 1989 Gobush et al. obtained a patent[14] for a golf ball that gave improved distance over the original icosahedron dimple pattern with 324 dimples. The improved distance was the direct result of making a golf ball with a particular aerodynamic configuration coupled with a particular spin velocity. The improved aerodynamic configuration was obtained by using the original icosahedron dimple pattern with about 384 ± 8 dimples. Titleist usually removed three dimples for the Titleist label and one dimple for the number on each pole. Thus, the dimple pattern was an icosahedron with 392 dimples minus eight dimples. The optimum dimple diameter was 0.145-0.155 inches and the optimum dimple depth was 0.0103-0.0123 inches. The desired spin velocity was accomplished by increasing the size of the golf ball's liquid center from 1 1/16 inch to 1 1/8 inch and by increasing the hardness of the cover. A harder cover resulted by using a balata cover made from at least 99% transpolyisoprene material instead of blending in cheaper softer rubbers such as gutta percha, butadiene, or natural rubber.

For a conventional golf ball having a nominal compression of between 90 and 100, the spin velocity varied between 3000 to about 3500 rpm when hit at 230 feet per second with a club face angle of 13 degrees. For the golf balls of this invention, the spin velocity was below 2900 rpm. A lower spin velocity resulted in a ball which had lower drag and a flatter trajectory. The combination of lower drag and a flatter trajectory resulted in a golf ball that had a longer carry distance and bounced and rolled further than a ball with a high trajectory. Lower spin also limited undesirable sidespin (hooking and slicing).

Actual distance testing data was obtained using a dual pendulum machine.[15] It is reported that Acushnet used an old Goodyear air dock—a shell built to manufacture dirigibles, to measure distances. This was 100 yards wide at the base, 300 yards long and 160 feet high.[16] The distance testing showed that the lower spin velocity and longer distance was a result of using the new dimple pattern (using 384 instead of 324 dimples), and of increasing the size of the liquid center (from 1 1/16 to 1/18 inch). In order to duplicate a driver, the ball was struck with an implement that had a 13 degree angle with respect to vertical, which gave a launch angle of 11 degrees. In order to duplicate a 5 iron, the ball was struck with an implement that had a 26 degree angle, which gave a launch angle of 21 degrees. The balata covered golf ball with 384 dimples and a core of 1 1/8 inch diameter had lower spin velocity and longer driver plus 5 iron distance (2799 rpm and 461.0 yards) than the balata covered golf ball with 324 dimples and a core of 1 1/16 inch diameter (3135 rpm and 447.6 yards).

Acushnet Company in 1983 announced the introduction of the new Titleist *384 TOUR 100* golf ball. The new golf ball was longer off the tee using the driver and was also longer using a 5 iron than any other golf ball on the PGA tour. The *384 TOUR 100* had longer carry distance and longer total distance than competing balls such as the Wilson T100 ball, the Golden Ram Pro Tour ball, the Hogan Apex 100 ball, and the MacGregor 100 ball.

The Titleist *384 TOUR 100* golf ball was a wound ball with a liquid center and a balata cover with 384 dimples. The *384 TOUR 100* ball was the same ball as the one described in Example 2 in the above mentioned patents[4-6]. So, I decided to determine whether the *384 TOUR 100* golf ball had a larger liquid center that was 1 1/8 inch in diameter. In order to determine this, I obtained a dental x-ray on the *384 TOUR 100* golf ball and compared this with the x-ray on the Pro Trajectory golf ball (Example 1 ball in Figure 2.11). The x-rays for the Pro Trajectory and the *384 TOUR 100* ball (proposed for Example 2) are shown in Figure 2.18.

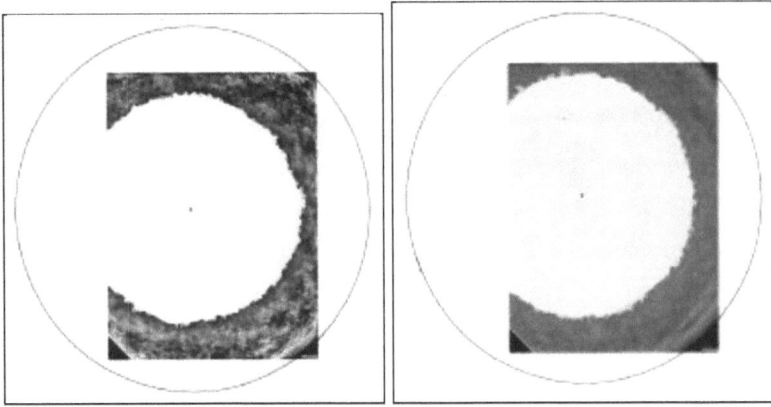

Figure 2.18 x-ray of Pro Trajectory ball #58 (left) and *384 TOUR 100* ball #3 (right)

These x-rays were obtained by placing the golf balls on the x-ray sensor fastened onto a flat surface and then taking the x-ray from above as discussed in Chapter 1. I determined the center of the golf ball by constructing two diameters on the center region using Thales Theorem[13]. The center of the golf ball is where the two diameters cross. Then using the center of the golf ball, I measured the diameter to the visible edge of the ball, which is set equal to 1.68 inches. The diameter of the liquid center of the golf ball can then be calculated. I calculated that the diameter of the liquid center of the *384 TOUR 100* golf ball was 1.11 inches (roughly 1 1/8 inches). The diameter of the liquid center of the Pro Trajectory ball was 1.02 inches (roughly 1 1/16 inches).

Other golf balls were also tested. For wound golf balls with a hard Surlyn ionomer[17] cover, longer distance could also be obtained by increasing the size of the core and the number of dimples from 1 1/16 inch and 324, to a ball with a 1 1/8 inch core and 384 dimples.

Surlyn covered golf balls were first patented in 1974 when Robert P. Molitor obtained a patent[18] for a superior golf ball cover composition that was cut and abrasion resistant, had better low temperature properties, and superior coefficient of restitution (CoR) properties. The Molitor invention consisted of mixing together a sodium ionic copolymer and a zinc ionic copolymer (Surlyn ionomers) obtained from du Pont Company, and then using this material to prepare the cover on a golf ball by injecting this material onto the golf ball core in the golf ball mold at elevated temperature and then cooling.

For a two-piece golf ball with a hard Surlyn ionomer cover, longer distance was also obtained by increasing the size of the core and the number of dimples from 1 1/16 inch and 324 dimples to 1 1/8 inch and 384 dimples. This data also shows that all things being equal, a two-piece ball traveled farther than a wound ball with a liquid center.

In 1971, Spalding became the first company to come out with a golf ball that had both a solid-core and a Surlyn cover.[19] They named the golf ball Top-Flite. Acushnet had obtained a British patent[12] for a golf ball with a solid core made of polybutadiene in 1974, but chose to use the Surlyn cover on the wound ball with a liquid center for the Titleist product line of golf balls.

Titleist golf balls with the original Icosahedron dimple pattern (384 IB)

Figure 2.19 *Titleist 7,* *384 Tour 100* golf ball #3 (384 IB)

Ball #3 (Figure 2.19) is a wound ball with a liquid center that has 384 dimples arranged in the original icosahedron dimple pattern (384 IB). A total of 8 dimples were removed for the name and the number. It was introduced in 1983 and had a balata cover. The liquid center for this ball had a diameter of 1 1/8 inches.

Figure 2.20 DT *Titleist 1,* *384 DT 90* golf ball #6 (384 IB)

Ball #6 (Figure 2.20) is a wound ball with a liquid center that has 384 dimples arranged in the original icosahedron dimple pattern (384 IB). A total of 8 dimples were removed for the name and the number. It was introduced in 1985 and had a Surlyn cover.

Figure 2.21 DT Titleist 3, *384 DT 90* golf ball #136 (384 IB)

Ball #136 (Figure 2.21) is the same as ball #6 above except it is yellow in color.

Figure 2.22 DT Titleist 2, *384 DT 90* golf ball #138 (384 IB)

Ball #138 (Figure 2.22) is the same as ball #6 above except it is orange in color.

Pinnacle Golf Ball with the 384 IB Dimple Pattern

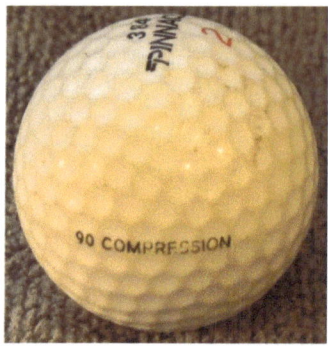

Figure 2.23 384 PINNACLE 2, 90 COMPRESSION ball #31 (384 IB)

Ball #31 (Figure 2.23) is a two-piece ball with 384 dimples arranged in the original icosahedron dimple pattern (384 IB). It had a balata cover.

Figure 2.24 384 PINNACLE 2, 90 COMPRESSION ball #100 (384 IB)

Ball #100 (Figure 2.24) is the same as ball #31 above except it is yellow in color.

Pinnacle Golf Ball with 392 IB Dimple Pattern

Figure 2.25 PINNACLE 4, 392 LS ball # 116 (392 IB)

Ball #116 (Figure 2.25) is a two-piece ball with 392 dimples arranged in the original icosahedron dimple pattern (392 IB). The dimples for the name and the number were not removed for this ball. It had a Surlyn cover.

Often, golf ball collectors have a difficult time determining the date that a vintage Titleist golf ball was first produced and sold. This is because golf ball manufacturers do not include any identifying numbers on the golf balls when they produce them. When I started my golf ball collection, I certainly had a difficult time dating golf balls. I realized that counting the number of dimples on a golf ball and inspecting the pattern the dimples make on the surface of a golf ball are almost the only things that one can determine visually. Therefore, examination of the dimple pattern on golf balls and counting the number of dimples are a reliable way to date a vintage golf ball. This can be done if you can match the dimple number and the dimple pattern on a vintage Titleist golf ball with the same dimple number and dimple pattern described in an Acushnet U.S. patent. The date that the U.S. patent was allowed (patents filed before 1995) or the date that the U.S. patent was filed (patents filed after 1995) becomes a reliable date that a vintage Titleist golf ball was first produced and sold.

Here is how I count the number of dimples on a golf ball. First, I locate the seam of the golf ball. All vintage Titleist golf balls have a seam—this is the part of the golf ball which is formed when the two cover halves are fused into one using the two molds that contain the dimple pattern. When the molds are removed, any excess cover material is then removed from the seam (equator) of the ball by grinding. Next, I take a water soluble marker (one that I use is made by Crayola®) and I count and mark each dimple starting from the seam and moving toward the pole of the golf ball. Then, I take the number of dimples on one hemisphere of the golf ball and multiply by two to get the total number of dimples on the golf ball. Finally, I wash off the water soluble marks on the surface of the golf ball. At first, this process was time consuming and tedious; however, with practice, I could determine the dimple pattern and dimple number quickly by inspection.

Synopsis Chapter Two

- Acushnet Company introduced two new icosahedron dimple patterns (324 IA) and (384 IB).
- These dimple patterns actually had 332 and 392 dimples except Acushnet Company removed 8 dimples for the golf ball name and number.
- The golf ball with the icosahedron dimple pattern traveled farther than the golf ball with the ATTI dimple pattern.
- A new durable cover made of Surlyn was introduced in 1974.
- Acushnet Company discovered that a golf ball with a large core plus a hard cover traveled farther and had lower spin.

- Golf ball performance testing was carried out using a dual pendulum machine.
- Golf balls with 384 dimples traveled farther than those with 324 dimples.
- Surlyn covered ball traveled farther than balata covered balls.
- Two-piece balls traveled farther than wound balls with a liquid center.

Chapter Three
Icosahedron with Dimples of Two Sizes
(392 IC)
Priority Date 1983

The invention of the original icosahedron dimple pattern in the 1970s was the first of many patents to appear concerning the dimples on Titleist golf balls. As I mentioned earlier, a patent gives the inventor an exclusive right to the technology for a period of time after the patent is allowed, and then the technology is free for anyone to use. A patent generally consists of the following parts: (1) Field of Invention, which in this case would be golf ball technology, (2) Background of Invention, which would include a description of the state of the art at the time the patent is filed, (3) Summary of Invention, which would describe in general terms the invention, (4) Detailed Description of Invention, which discloses all relevant parts of the invention, including broad embodiments, preferred embodiments, and most preferred embodiments, (5) Examples, which would show data used to support the invention, and (6) Claims, which actually are the legally binding parts of the invention that the inventor claims.

The next new dimple pattern appeared in 1989 when Gobush et al obtained a series of patents[1-5] for a golf ball that traveled further than golf balls on the market then without violating any of the rules promulgated by the USGA. The Gobush patents taught that the USGA had two static tests for golf balls: first, the weight of a golf ball should not exceed 1.620 ounces; and second, the size of a golf ball shall not be less than 1.680 inches. There were also three performance tests for golf balls at that time. First, a golf ball may not exceed a velocity of 250 ± 2% feet per second when measured on a device approved by the USGA. Second, a golf ball may not exceed a distance of 280 ± 6% yards when struck by a driver. The overall distance is the sum of the carry distance plus the roll distance. Third, a golf ball shall be designed and manufactured to perform as if it were spherically symmetrical.

Figure 3.1 Polara golf ball

In 1975, the PGA/Victor Company produced a golf ball called the Polara® (Figure 3.1). The Polara would fly straight without violating any USGA rules in force at that time. This ball was smooth at the poles and had a band of dimples around the equator. This geometry caused the Polara ball to right itself in flight, minimizing the slice and hook trajectories that were problems for many recreational golfers. The USGA refused to approve this ball because they decided the ball would drastically change the way golf was played. In 1981 the USGA adopted the symmetry rule, which stated that a ball must not be designed, manufactured, or modified to have properties that differed from those of a spherically symmetrical ball.

The Gobush patents disclosed a golf ball that traveled further by covering the golf ball with dimples of at least two different sizes. The dimples were arranged in an icosahedron pattern containing twenty triangular regions. Small dimples were located at the vertices and the edges of the triangular regions and large dimples were located inside the triangular regions. For a ball with 392 dimples, the smaller dimples (labeled 10, 12, and 18) had a diameter of 0.140 inches and the larger dimples (labeled 14) had a diameter of 0.160 inches. This dimple pattern (392 IC, stands for 392 dimples, icosahedron pattern C) is shown in Figure 3.2, which is the polar region for the golf ball with two different size dimples.

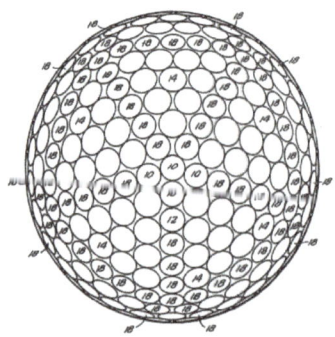

Figure 3.2 Golf ball with 392 IC dimple pattern[1]

The isometric views for the golf balls with the original icosahedron pattern with 392 dimples of one size (original icosahedron in Figure 3.3) and for the icosahedron with 392 dimples of two sizes (392 IC in Figure 3.4) are compared below. In Figure 3.4, the blue colored dimples are the smaller dimples.

In Figure 3.3 the dimples adjacent to the equator or seam of the golf ball are directly opposite the dimples located in the row below the equator. In Figure 3.4, the dimples next to the equator are not directly opposite the dimples located in the row below the equator, but rather they are located in between two dimples located in the row below the equator. Figure 3.3 can be converted into Figure 3.4 by rotating the southern hemisphere a total of three and a half dimples to the right (42 degrees) with respect to the northern hemisphere.

While the equatorial region of Figure 3.3 does not look very much like a regular icosahedron, the equatorial region of Figure 3.4 does look like a slightly skewed regular icosahedron. I believe this change in the dimple pattern from Figure 3.3 to 3.4 was necessary because of the new 1981 USGA symmetry rule, which stated that a golf ball shall be designed and manufactured to perform in general as if it were spherically symmetric. The golf ball with the original icosahedron pattern (Figure 3.3) may not be considered spherically symmetric. The skewed icosahedron of Figure 3.4 more closely resembles a regular icosahedron and may perform as if it were spherically symmetric.

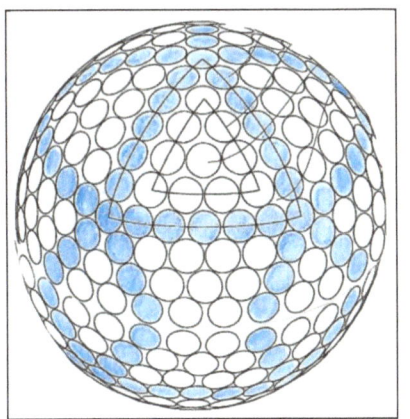 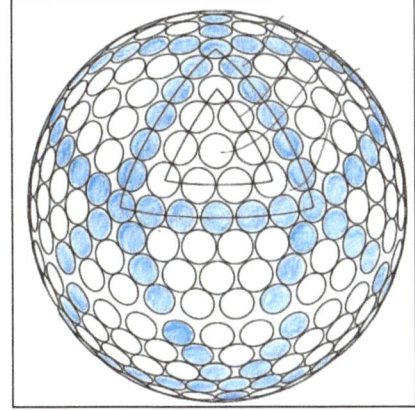

Figure 3.3 Original Icosahedron Pattern **Figure 3.4** Two Size Dimple Pattern

Five different sets of dimple patterns were disclosed for the golf balls with different size dimples. They included two size dimple pattern having a total of 332, 392, 422, and 492 dimples, and a triple size dimple pattern having a total of 492 dimples. In all cases, eight dimples could be removed for the name and number if desired. These patents taught that if the total surface area of the golf ball covered with dimples exceeded 78% of the total surface area, the golf ball would travel a substantially greater distance than if the surface coverage was lower. In other words, improved aerodynamics results in improved distance, and minimizing the surface area not covered with dimples resulted in improved aerodynamics. The dimple pattern shown in Figure 3.4 was the one used to exceed 78% coverage.

The comparison of the percent dimple coverage on the surface for golf balls with one size dimples versus two sizes of dimples is shown in Figure 3.5 for golf balls with 324, 384, 414, and 484 dimples. The golf balls with two size dimples had greater than 78% dimple coverage and the golf balls with only one size dimple had less than 78% dimple coverage in all cases.

TABLE V

Pattern Number	Total Number of Dimples	Number Dimples at Different Diameter	Dimple Diameter	Percent Dimple Coverage
1	324	324	0.157	70.7
2	324	124	0.157	
		200	0.170	78.3
3	384	384	0.146	72.5
4	384	144	0.140	
		240	0.160	79.4
5	414	414	0.140	71.9
6	414	270	0.150	
		144	0.140	78.8
7	484	484	0.130	72.5
8	484	174	0.130	
		310	0.140	79.9
9	484	174	0.130	
		260	0.140	
		50	0.150	81.2

Figure 3.5 Percent Dimple Coverage for various dimple patterns[2]

If you think about it, removing dimples for the name and the number on the golf ball results in a ball that has fewer dimples and therefore must have lower percent surface coverage than one where those dimples were not removed. I calculated the percent surface coverage for golf balls with 324 versus 332 dimples and for golf balls with 384 versus 392 dimples. Since the dimples removed for the name and the number are all small dimples (see Figure 3.2), a golf ball with 332 dimples would have 132 dimples with a diameter of 0.157 inches and 200 dimples with a diameter of 0.170 inches (see Figure 3.5). This gives 80.0% coverage compared to 78.3% coverage for the ball with dimples removed. Likewise the golf ball with 392 dimples would have 152 dimples with a diameter of 0.140 inches and 240 dimples with a diameter of 0.160 inch which gives 80.8% coverage. This is greater than 79.4% for the ball with 324 dimples reported in Figure 3.5. Also, removing dimples at the poles for the name and the number may affect the spherical symmetry of the golf ball. It turns out, probably because of this Acushnet Company no longer removed the dimples for the name and the number from Titleist and Pinnacle golf balls from that time forward.

Dimple Profile

The dimple profile on a golf ball was also an important factor for the golf balls of this invention. Dimple profile is a combination of at least three parameters: the shape of the dimple (circular, square, triangular, or other), the dimple diameter (distance from one edge to another), and the dimple depth D (distance from deepest part of the dimple to the periphery line of the surface). The way to measure the dimple depth (D) and dimple diameter for the dimples with a spherical profile of the present invention is shown in Figure 3.6 below.

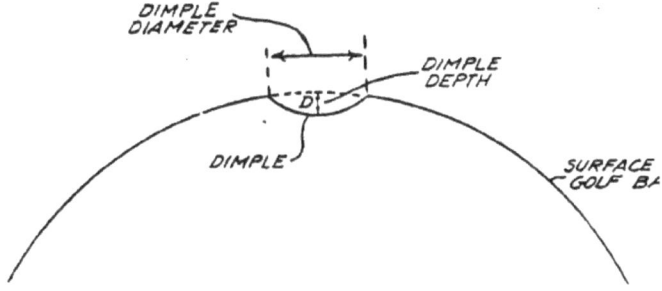

Figure 3.6 Definition of dimple diameter and dimple depth[3]

The preferred dimple diameters for all the different dimple patterns of this invention with two different size dimples is shown in Figure 3.7.

Total Number of Dimples	First Set Nominal Dimple Diameter (inches)	Second Set Nominal Dimple Diameter (inches)
324	0.157	0.17
332	0.157	0.17
384	0.14	0.16
392	0.14	0.16
384	0.13	0.16
392	0.13	0.16
414	0.14	0.15
422	0.14	0.15
484	0.13	0.14
492	0.13	0.14

Figure 3.7 Preferred dimple diameters for a golf ball with different numbers of dimples[5]

Performance testing the two size dimple pattern golf ball

A two piece golf ball with 384 dimples made with 144 small dimples (0.140 inch diameter, 0.0110 inch depth) and 240 large dimples (0.160 inch diameter, 0.0010 depth) was tested using a dual pendulum machine and against a two piece golf ball with 384 dimples made with only one size dimple (0.150 inch diameter, 0.0115 depth). The results showed that the ball with dimples of two sizes traveled farther 380.3 yards total carry + roll than the golf ball with only one size dimple, which traveled 374.2 yards total carry + roll.

Golf Ball for the Average Golfer

The golf balls with dimples of two sizes (392 IC dimple pattern), a solid rubber center with a diameter of 1 1/8 inches, and a hard Surlyn cover were named the Titleist DT golf balls. They flew farther and had lower spin than previous golf balls. The Titleist DT was the ball of choice for the average golfer who wanted longer distance and lower spin. Lower spin helped reduce the unwanted hook and slice that the average golfer found difficult to control. The harder Surlyn cover was tolerable because it was more durable and resisted cutting and abrasion.

The terminology 'DT' can be confusing. Initially, 'DT' on a Titleist golf ball meant 'dynamite thread' which was introduced in about 1948. Then, 'DT' meant durable Titleist, which referred to the more durable Surlyn covers that were introduced in 1974. Finally, the Titleist DT stood for Distance Titleist. This ball became an important product for Acushnet and is still produced even today.

Photographs of Titleist Golf Balls with Dimple of Two Sizes
Titleist DT Golf Balls with 392 IC Dimple Pattern

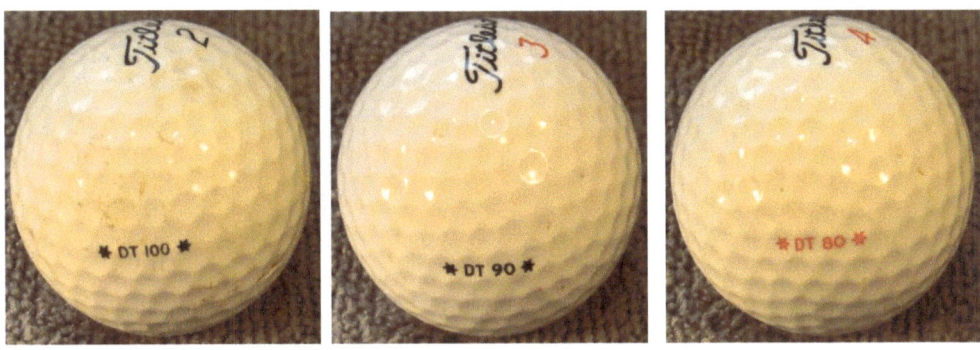

Figure 3.8 Titleisst DT 100, 90, and 80 golf balls #8 (left), #77 (middle), and #94 (right)

Balls #8, #77, and #94 (Figure 3.8) were wound balls with a solid rubber center and a Surlyn cover. They had 392 dimples in two sizes arranged in the 392 IC dimple pattern. They were made with three different compressions, 80, 90 and 100. I believe that these golf balls were first released in 1991.[6]

Figure 3.9 Titleist DT 90 golf ball #90

Ball #90 (Figure 3.9) has lower compression and has a slightly different seam marking than ball #77 above. This is an indication that ball #90 was produced a few years after ball #77.

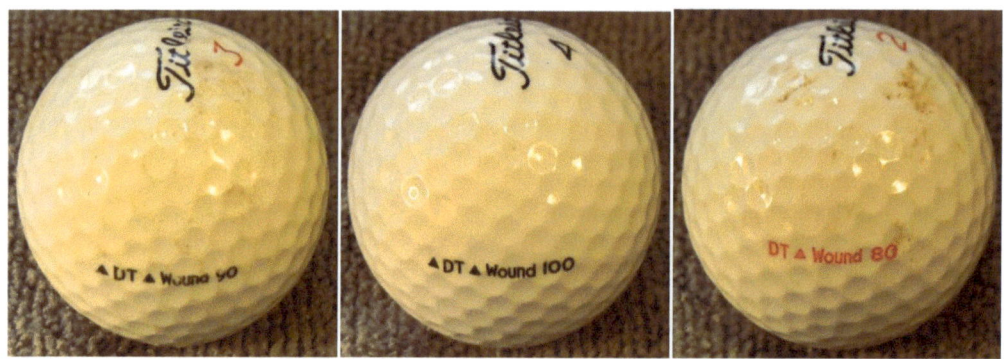

Figure 3.10 Titleist DT Wound golf balls #9 (left), #52 (center), and #95 (right)

The Titleist DT wound golf balls #9, #52, and #95 (Figure 3.10) are all wound balls with a solid center and a Surlyn cover. They had 392 dimples in two sizes arranged in the 392 IC dimple pattern. These golf balls were first introduced in 1996.[6]

Figure 3.11 Titleist DT Distance golf ball #19

The Titleist DT Distance ball #19 (Figure 3.11) is a two-piece ball with a Surlyn cover that has 392 dimples arranged in the 392 IC pattern. This ball was first introduced in 2000.[6]

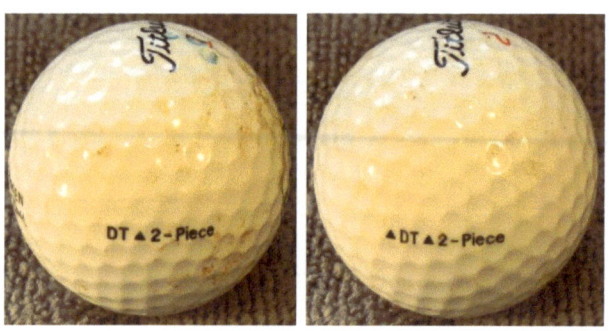

Figure 3.12 Titleist DT 2-Piece golf balls #10 (left) and #49 (right)

The Titleist DT 2-Piece golf balls #10 and #49 (Figure 3.12) are two-piece golf balls with a Surlyn cover that have 392 dimples arranged in the 392 IC pattern. This ball was first introduced in 1996.[6]

Golf Ball for Professional Golfer

Professional golfers prefer a ball that has the usual click and feel of a liquid center wound ball, and also has higher spin. The professional golfer found this desirable because they had more control on approach shots to the green. The liquid center wound golf balls with softer covers for the professional included the Titleist Tour golf ball, the Titleist Tour Balata golf ball, the Titleist Professional golf ball, and the Titleist Pro V1 392. The Tour ball and the Tour Balata ball were liquid center wound balls with 392 dimples arranged in the 392 IC pattern with a balata cover. The Tour Balata ball, which was produced from 1994-2000,[6] had an improved winding process that reduced the breakage of threads about the liquid center.[7] The Professional, which was produced from 1995-2001,[6] was a liquid center wound ball with dimples arranged in the 392 IC pattern and a urethane elastomer (polyurethane) cover. The urethane elastomer cover was almost as durable as the Surlyn cover and was almost as soft as balata.

Here are some photos of the golf balls in my collection that have 392 dimples in two sizes that were widely used by professional golfers in the 1990s. These were wound balls with liquid centers that had the spin, click and soft feel that the professional golfers preferred.

Titleist TOUR golf balls with 392 IC Dimple Pattern

Figure 3.13 Tour golf balls #15 (left) and #131 (right)

The Tour golf balls #15 and #131 (Figure 3.13) are wound golf balls with a liquid center and a balata cover that contained 392 dimples arranged in the 392 IC pattern. These golf balls were introduced in 1991.[6]

Titliest Professional Golf Balls with 392 IC Dimple Pattern

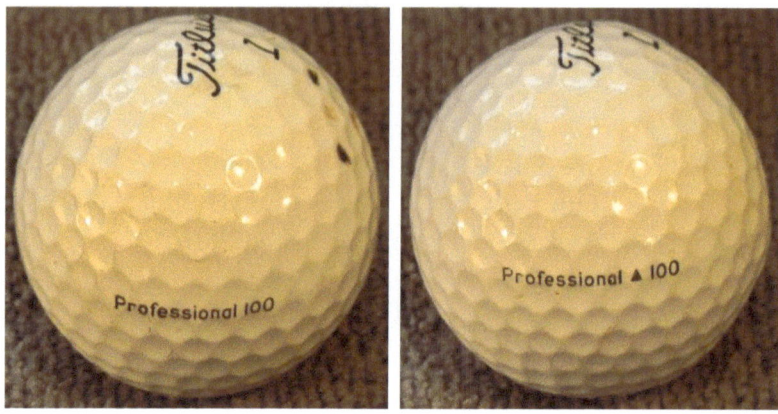

Figure 3.14 Professional 100 golf balls #86 (left) and #164 (right)

Figure 3.15 Professional 90 golf balls #134 (left) and #5 (right)

The Professional golf balls #86, #164 (Figure 3.14) and #134, and #5 (Figure 3.15) are wound balls with a liquid center and a polyurethane cover. These golf balls have 392 dimples arranged in the 392 IC pattern. The Professional golf ball was first introduced in 1995.[6]

Titleist Tour Balata Golf Balls with 392 IC Dimple Pattern

Figure 3.16 Tour Balata golf balls #135 (left) and #70 (right)

The Tour Balata golf balls #135 and #70 (Figure 3.16) are wound balls with a liquid center and a balata cover. They were first introduced in 1994.[6]

Titleist Tour Distance Golf Balls with 392 IC Dimple Pattern

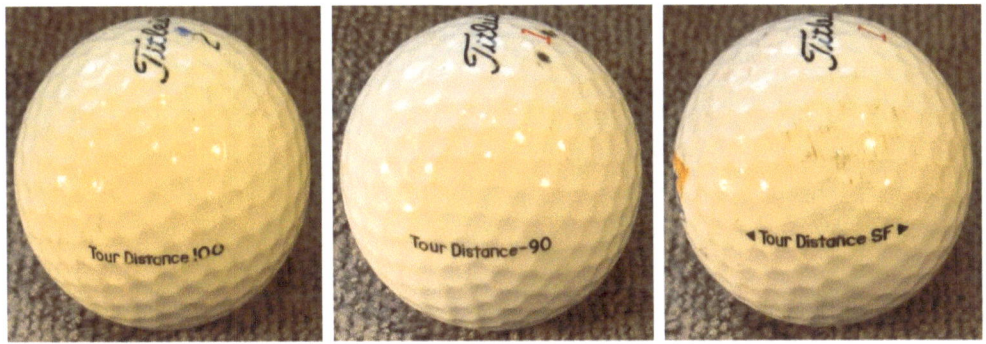

Figure 3.17 Titleist Tour Distance golf balls #16 (left), #40 (center), and #21 (right)

The Titleist Tour Distance golf balls #16, #40, and #21 (Figure 3.17) are two-piece balls with a Surlyn cover that had 392 dimples arranged in the 392 IC pattern. The Tour Distance ball was introduced in 1998 and the Tour Distance SF was introduced in 2001.[6]

Titleist Pro V1 Golf Balls with 392 IC Dimple Pattern

Figure 3.18 Titleist Pro V1 392 golf balls #18 (left) and #42 (right)

The first Titleist Pro V1 392 golf balls, #18 and #42 (Figure 3.18) were introduced in 1999 and 2001[6] respectively. Both golf balls are three-piece golf balls that had one solid core and two covers.[8] The Pro V1 golf balls immediately became very popular because they traveled a long distance, had a soft feel, a durable cover, and high spin rate. This was made possible by combining a low spin construction (a polybutadiene core and a hard inner cover) with a very thin soft outer cover (thermoset polyurethane).

The golf balls produced in the early 1990s could be made with a liquid center or a solid rubber center, they could be wound or two-piece, and the covers could be made from balata, Surlyn ionomer, or polyurethane elastomer. Combined with the production of three different compressions (80, 90, and 100), the possible number of golf balls that could be produced is quite large. One reference states that in 1992, Titleist/Pinnacle had 72 different golf ball varieties on the USGA conforming ball list, while in 1996 they had about 180.[9]

Photographs of Pinnacle Golf Balls with 392 IC Dimple Pattern

These are Pinnacle golf balls that have the 392 IC dimple pattern. These golf balls are all two-piece balls with a Surlyn cover.

Figure 3.19 Pinnacle golf balls #71 (left), # 72 (center), and #93 (right)

Figure 3.20 Pinnacle golf balls #32 (left) and #249 (right)

Figure 3.21 Pinnacle golf balls #106 (left) and #171 (right)

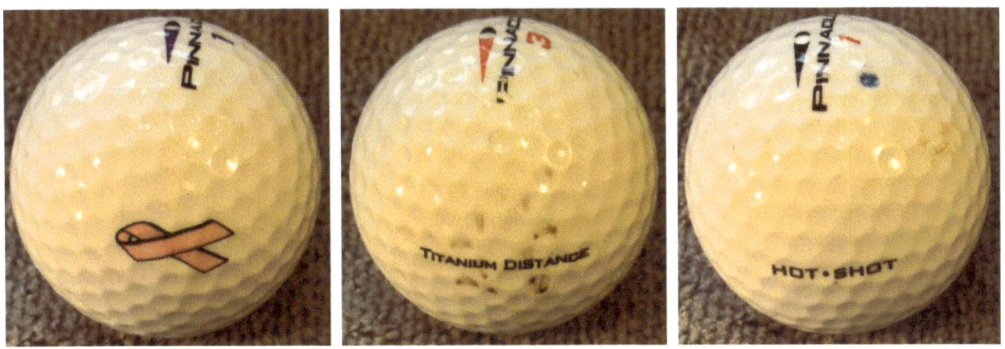

Figure 3.22 Pinnacle golf balls #174 (left), #178 (center), and #181 (right)

Synopsis Chapter Three
- USGA established rules for golf ball size, weight, initial velocity, overall distance, and symmetry that every golf ball must meet.

- Acushnet Company introduced a new icosahedron dimple pattern with 392 dimples of 2-sizes (392 IC).
- The increased distance of golf balls with the 392 IC dimple pattern was due primarily to an increase in the dimple percent surface coverage.
- The average golfer preferred a two-piece golf ball with a hard Surlyn cover because it had low spin, traveled far, and was durable.
- The professional golfer preferred a wound ball with liquid center, high spin, and good 'click and feel.'
- Acushnet Company introduced a new polyurethane cover process.
- The very first Pro V1 392 was a three-piece ball with two covers, and it had soft feel, long distance, and high spin rate.

CHAPTER FOUR
OCTAHEDRAL DIMPLE PATTERNS
(440 CO, 416 OQ)
PRIORITY DATE 1989

While Gobush was developing the successful 392 IC dimple pattern based on an icosahedron pattern, Aoyama, another scientist at Acushnet Company, was looking at golf ball dimple patterns based on variations of an octahedron. The first new dimple pattern, patented in 1990[1], was one based on a cuboctahedron. A cuboctahedron is a polyhedron with six square faces and eight triangular faces. Here is an orthographic projection for a cuboctahedron[2].

Figure 4.1 Orthographic projection of a cuboctahedron[2]

The USGA had promulgated rules requiring that a golf ball must perform generally as if it were spherically symmetrical. The cuboctahedron dimple pattern met this rule. The cuboctahedral golf ball had four parting lines (great circular paths that encircle the golf ball) where none of the parting lines intersected any of the dimples. The dimples were evenly and uniformly distributed over the surface of the golf ball inside each of the six squares and in each of the eight equilateral triangles making sure that none of the dimples intersected any of the common edges. At least about 65% of the surface was covered with dimples. Each square and each triangle had the same dimple pattern as every other square and triangle respectively. The preferred dimple patterns had a total of 408, 432, or 456 dimples.

Cuboctahedral golf ball with 456 dimples, two sizes

The triangular and square regions for the golf ball with 456 dimples are shown in Figure 4.2. There were two different dimple sizes labeled 72 and 76 in Figure 4.2. There were 168 dimples in the eight triangular regions that had a maximum diameter of about 0.136 inch, and there were 288 dimples in the six square regions that had a maximum dimple diameter of about 0.139 inch. I calculate[3] that 76.9% of the surface of this ball was covered with dimples.

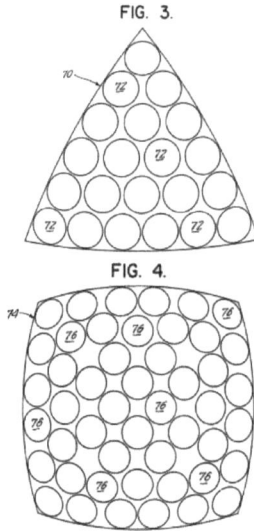

Figure 4.2 Dimple pattern for triangular and square regions, cuboctahedral ball, 456 dimples[1]

The six square regions and the eight triangular regions were positioned on the surface of the golf ball to form a cuboctahedral pattern as shown in Figure 4.3.

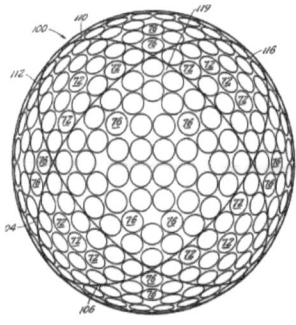

Figure 4.3 Cuboctahedron pattern for ball with 456 dimples[1]

Cuboctahedron Dimple Pattern with Higher Lift to Drag Ratio

In 1990, Aoyama obtained a patent[4] for a golf ball with a cuboctahedron dimple pattern that contained dimples of many sizes. This patent taught that one could obtain a higher lift to drag ratio if the dimples were arranged on the surface of the golf ball so no three dimples in a row had edges that aligned. It was believed that this configuration resulted in a golf ball with a lower coefficient of drag. Scientists at Acushnet Company had begun to study the aerodynamics of dimples on a golf ball and they theorized that a higher lift to drag ratio meant this golf ball could be made to travel farther. The preferred dimple pattern had 440 dimples. Figure 4.4 illustrates an example where there are three dimples in a row with edges not aligned.

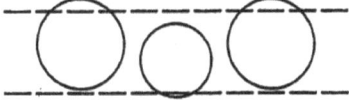

Figure 4.4 Three dimples in a row with edges not aligned.[4]

The triangular and square regions for the golf ball with 440 dimples, where the edges of three dimples in a row are not aligned, are shown in Figure 4.5. This ball had a total of twelve different size dimples. The smallest size dimple had a diameter of 0.090 inch and the largest size dimple had a diameter of 0.170 inch.

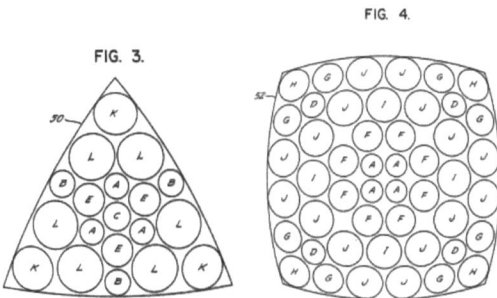

Figure 4.5 Dimple pattern for triangular and square regions, cuboctahedral ball, 440 dimples[4]

One of the preferred sets of dimple diameter and dimple depth for the cuboctahedral ball with 440 dimples is shown in Figure 4.6. I calculate[3] the percent coverage for the golf ball with 440 dimples was 70.7%.

TABLE I

Type	(FIG. 3 and 4) Diameter (inches)	Depth (inches)
A	0.090	0.0071
B	0.095	0.0075
C	0.100	0.0079
D	0.105	0.0083
E	0.115	0.0091
F	0.125	0.0099
G	0.130	0.0102
H	0.140	0.0110
I	0.145	0.0114
J	0.150	0.0118
K	0.160	0.0126
L	0.170	0.0134

Figure 4.6 Dimple diameter and dimple depth for cuboctahedral ball, 440 dimples.[4]

Flight test results obtained with a dual pendulum driving machine, compared the distance traveled by the new cuboctahedron golf ball that had 440 dimples with the older Titleist 384 DT golf ball. The Titleist 384 DT golf ball had a larger wound liquid center and a Surlyn cover discussed in Chapter 3. The cuboctahedron golf ball with 440 dimples in this comparison was a wound ball with a liquid center and a Surlyn cover.

Distance test results show that the cuboctahedron ball with 440 dimples (Fig. 7 in reference 4) traveled 7.3 yards farther than the 384 DT ball when struck with a driver with an 11 degree loft angle, and traveled 2.3 yards farther than the 384 DT ball when struck with a driver with a 13 degree loft angle. Interestingly, when struck with a driver with a 15 degree loft angle, or when struck with an iron with a 26 degree loft angle, the 384 DT ball traveled farther. The cuboctahedron ball with 440 dimples traveled farther when hit by a driver or a club with a low loft angle, but did not travel as far when hit by an iron or a club with a high loft angle. It turns out the reason for this is that some of the dimples are too small. A later patent[5] disclosed that filling the surface of a golf ball with small dimples in order to get higher dimple coverage was not very effective because tiny dimples were not good turbulence generators. Ultimately a minimum dimple diameter of about 0.11 inches was chosen for the smallest dimple diameter.

An image of the golf ball having 440 dimples is shown in Figure 4.7. This dimple pattern appears on the following golf balls in my collection: *HVC 100* (ball #37), *HVC 90* (ball #153), HVC TOUR (ball #36), HP2 Tour (ball #166), HP2

Δ TOUR (ball #35), HP2 Δ 100 (ball #51), HP2 Δ 90 (ball #84), HP2 Δ Distance (ball #82), and HP2 Distance (ball #167).

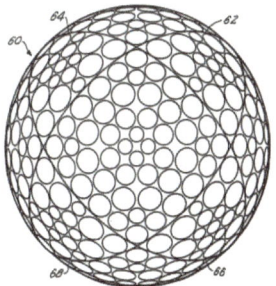

Figure 4.7 Cuboctahedron golf ball[4]

The *HVC 100* ball, introduced in 1991, was a two-piece ball with a solid core made from crosslinked polybutadiene polymer, instead of a wound ball with a liquid center. This ball is reported to be the first two-piece Titleist golf ball to ever bear the Titleist script.[6] Additional information about the core and the cover, which cannot be determined by inspection, can be learned about the HVC technology by examining the original golf ball packaging information that contained the Titleist HVC golf balls. On the box cover of the HVC Δ 90 golf ball, there is a list of the U.S. patents that cover the HVC technology. Using this information I learned that Titleist made improvements in its original solid core technology that was patented[7] in 1971. Later, Titleist patented the new high velocity core in 1985[8]. Titleist also made improvements in its original ionomer cover technology[9] (Na and Zn Surlyn ionomeric resins) and patented the new cover for the *HVC 100* ball using Na and Li Surlyn ionomeric resins.[10] Golf ball collectors should take good care of golf ball boxes so they can find relevant U.S. patents that disclose information about the golf balls.

Photographs of Titleist Golf Balls with 440 CO Dimple Pattern

Figure 4.8 Titleist HVC golf Balls #36 (left), #153 (center), and #37 (right)

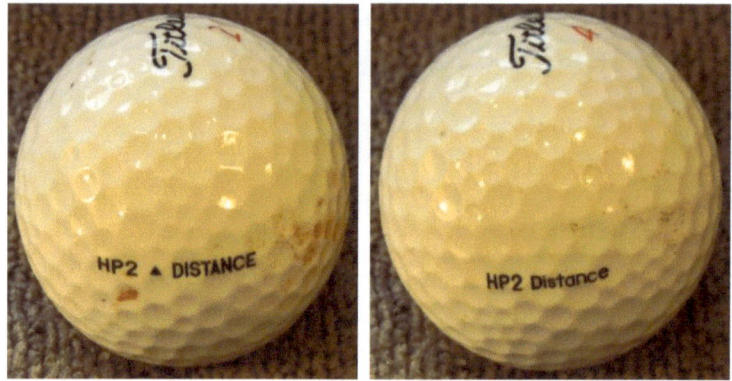

Figure 4.9 Titleist HP2 golf Balls, #82 (left) and # 167 (right)

Figure 4.10 Titleist HP2 Tour golf Balls #35 (left) and #166 (right)

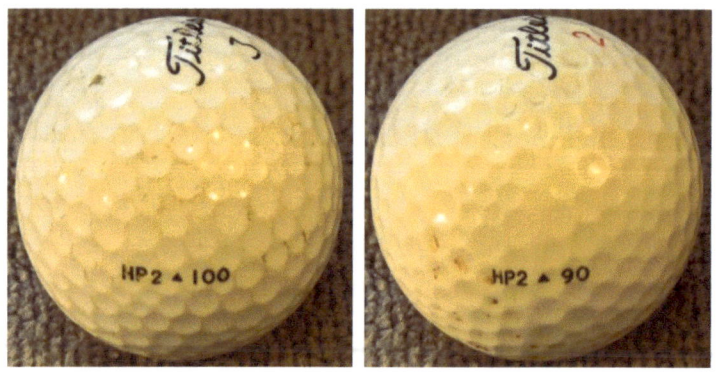

Figure 4.11 Titleist HP2 golf Balls #51 (left) and #84 (right)

Pinnacle golf balls with the 440 CO Dimple Pattern

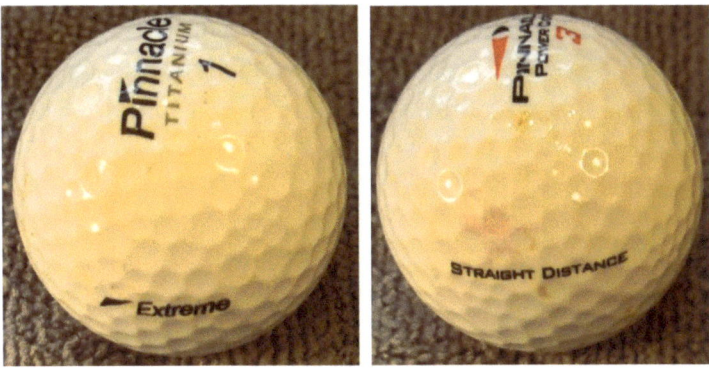

Figure 4.12 Pinnacle golf balls #113 (left) and #175 (right)

These golf balls were not very popular among recreational and professional golfers. Many recreational golfers liked the extra distance of the two-piece construction and the lack of spin, but the ball felt too hard. Professional golfers liked the extra distance but did not like the reduced spin that these ball offered and preferred the so called 'click and feel' of the liquid center wound golf ball construction.

Different dimple profiles on the same ball

In 1992, Aoyama obtained a patent[11] for a golf ball that not only had multiple sets of dimples with different diameters, but also had a different dimple profile for each set. Some of the sets had dimples with a spherical shape profile (labeled 11, Fig. 2) and other sets of dimples had a saucer shaped profile (labeled 12, Fig. 2). Up until this time, all golf balls had dimples with the same shape profile. This resulted in an improvement in the aerodynamic effectiveness of each dimple size. The edge angle was defined as the angle (e) made by a tangent at the circumference of the ball (T^1) and a tangent at the edge of the dimple (T_2) at point P as shown in Figure 4.13.

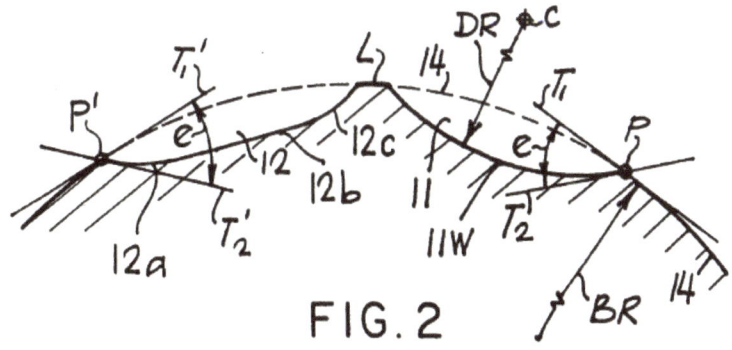

Figure 4.13 Two dimple profiles—saucer shaped (12) and spherical shaped (11)[11]

Regular Octahedron Quadrilateral Pattern

In 1995, Aoyama obtained a patent[12] for a golf ball with a regular octahedral[13] dimple pattern comprising eight spherical triangles bordered by three great circle parting lines that did not intersect any dimples. One parting line was at the equator of the ball and two parting lines passed through each pole.

Figure 4.14 Orthographic projection of a regular octahedron

Each spherical triangle was formed from three quadrilaterals having identical dimple patterns that were angularly spaced at 120 degrees from one another and centered in the spherical triangles, resulting in a total of twenty-four equivalent quadrilaterals on the spherical surface. The patent disclosed two examples of quadrilaterals with identical dimple patterns that contained either 384 dimples or 456 dimples. Figure 4.15 shows the three identical quadrilaterals that made up one spherical triangle for the octahedral golf ball with 456 total dimples. Each quadrilateral contained 57 dimples of multiple sizes with the smallest dimple diameter equal to 0.100 inch and the largest dimple equal to 0.160 inch. As you can see, two dimples are shared by each of two different quadrilaterals.

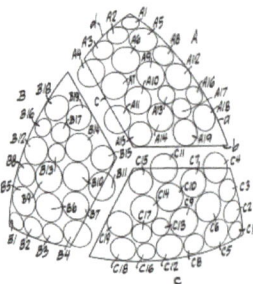

Figure 4.15 Three equivalent quadrilaterals on the regular octahedral ball with 456 dimples.[12]

The number of dimples and the dimple diameter for the golf ball with the octahedral dimple pattern and 456 dimples is shown in Figure 4.16. I calculate the percent coverage for this ball to be 75.9%.

GOLF BALL COVER STORY

TABLE I	
Number of Dimples	Dimple Diameter
72	.100 in.
24	.110 in.
72	.120 in.
24	.130 in.
48	.140 in.
120	.150 in.
96	.160 in.

Figure 4.16 Dimple number and dimple diameter for octahedral ball with 456 dimples.[12]

In my golf ball collection, I have four golf balls that have a total of 416 dimples in an octahedral dimple pattern that consists of eight triangular regions composed of three equivalent quadrilaterals. I believe that these golf balls fall within claim 1 of reference 5, the broadest claim, but are not specifically disclosed in the application. So I decided to figure out what the dimple pattern was for the quadrilaterals used in these golf balls. The golf balls were the < HP > (ball #141), < HP ∘ Distance > (ball #54), the HVC Soft Feel (ball #81), and the < HP TOUR > (ball #80). Here is my drawing (Figure 4.17) for the dimple pattern for these two golf balls. In this quadrilateral, there are sixteen dimples in each quadrilateral region, two dimples are shared by each of two different quadrilaterals and one dimple is shared by three quadrilaterals. There are a total of 52 dimples in each triangular region of the regular octahedron and about six different dimple sizes.

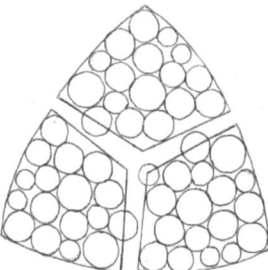

Figure 4.17 My Drawing for the 416 dimple quadrilateral based octahedron

Titleist golf balls with the 416 QO Dimple Pattern

Figure 4.18 Titleist HP golf Balls #141 (left), #80 (center), #54 (right)

Figure 4.19 Titleist HVC Soft Feel golf Ball #81

Hybrid Dimple Pattern—Octahedron plus Icosahedron

In 2005, William E. Morgan and Steven Aoyama obtained a patent[13] for a golf ball that had two different dimple patterns arranged in two distinct regions. In a preferred embodiment, the polar region contained an octahedron dimple pattern, and the equatorial region contained an icosahedron dimple pattern. There were a total of 388 dimples arranged in eight sizes. The patent taught that most icosahedron-based dimple patterns had more densely packed dimples located near the pole than near the equator. This resulted in a ball that tended to fly slightly lower and longer in the poles-horizontal (PH) position than in the pole-over-pole (PP) position. This was bad news for the icosahedron-based dimple pattern, because this golf ball would not meet the USGA symmetry requirement. The inventors found that if they designed a golf ball that had an octahedron dimple pattern in the polar region and an icosahedron dimple pattern in the equatorial region, the ball would fly consistently regardless of orientation. This golf ball is shown in Figure 4.20.

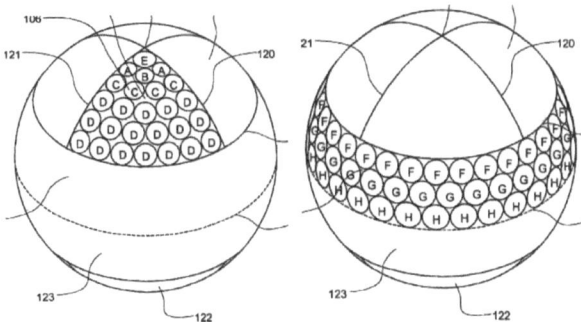

Figure 4.20 Golf ball with polar octahedron pattern and equatorial icosahedron dimple pattern[13]

This golf ball had a total of eight different size dimples, five sizes for the octahedron region (Figure 4.21) and three sizes for the icosahedron region Figure 4.22) There are no golf balls in my collection that have this dimple pattern.

TABLE 3

Dimple	Diameter (in.)
A	0,115
B	0.120
C	0.130
D	0.145
E	0.150

Figure 4.21 Dimple sizes for the octahedron region (polar region)[13]

TABLE 4

Dimple	Diameter (in.)
F	0.155
G	0.165
H	0,170

Figure 4.22 Dimples sizes for the icosahedron region (equatorial region)[13]

Synopsis Chapter Four

- Two new octahedral dimple patterns were introduced which were more symmetric than the icosahedral dimple pattern.

- One new pattern, a cuboctahedral pattern (440 CO), was composed of six square and eight triangular regions.
- These octahedral dimple patterns obeyed the USGA symmetry rule.
- A golf ball had a higher lift to drag ratio if no three dimple edges were aligned.
- The HVC golf ball was the first Titleist two-piece ball.
- This two-piece golf ball had low spin rate and felt hard.
- Dimples improve the aerodynamics as long as they are of a reasonable size (>0.11 inch).
- The 416 OQ dimple pattern was an octahedral pattern; wherein, each of the eight triangular regions were made from three equivalent quadrilaterals.
- Improved performance results when dimples have two different edge angles on the same ball.

Chapter Five
Dimples of Multiple Sizes
(392 ID)
Priority Date 1997

In 1999 and 2002, Aoyama obtained patents[1-2] for a golf ball with dimples of multiple sizes. Dimples on a golf ball create a turbulent boundary layer around the ball that helps the turbulent boundary layer to stay attached further around the ball and reduces the area of the wake. This increases the pressure behind the ball, which reduces the drag. A high degree of dimple coverage is beneficial to flight distance but only if the dimples are of a reasonable size. Very small dimples are not good turbulence generators, so incorporation of very small dimples (<0.10 inch diameter) on the surface of a golf ball does not create enough turbulence at average golf ball velocities.

The golf ball with dimples of multiple sizes had better dimple packing than previous dimple patterns. The surface of this golf ball had a higher surface coverage of dimples. The surface coverage was greater than 80%! This was achieved by using five or more dimple sizes and by arranging the dimples in a series of triangular regions on the surface.

Icosahedron, 362 dimples, 5 sizes

The first embodiment of this invention was a golf ball with a regular icosahedron dimple pattern made from 362 dimples. This was an example of a truly regular icosahedron. This ball did not have a great circle (seam) that did not intersect any dimples. This increased the percentage of the surface that was covered by dimples but made manufacturing more difficult, because now there was one row of dimples directly at the seam (equator) of the golf ball. It is very difficult to remove the excess cover material from the seam when it is covered with dimples. The polar region and the equatorial region of the icosahedron golf ball with 362 multiple size dimples are shown in Figure 5.1. There were five different sizes of dimples labeled A through E.

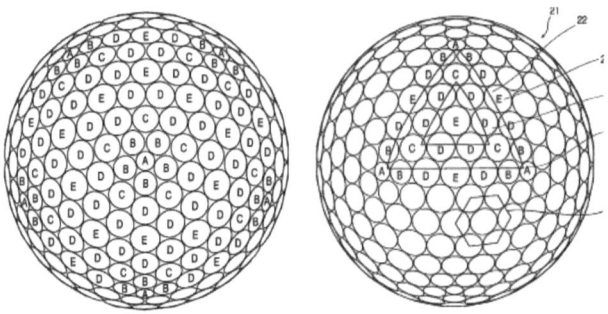

Figure 5.1 Polar (left) and equatorial (right) regions of Icosahedron with 362 dimples, 5 sizes.[1]

The preferred dimple sizes for the regular icosahedron ball with 362 dimples are shown in Figure 5.2 (Table 1 in reference 1)

TABLE 1

Dimple	Diameter (inches)
A	.11
B	.14
C	.16
D	.17
E	.18

Figure 5.2 Dimple sizes for Icosahedron with 362 dimples[1]

Altogether, I count there are 12 dimples labeled A, 60 dimples labeled B, 60 dimples labeled C, 180 dimples labeled D, and 50 dimples labeled E on the ball with 362 dimples. My calculations[3] indicate that this ball has 85.9 % surface coverage. I do not have any golf balls in my collection that have this dimple pattern

Icosahedron, 392 dimples, 5 sizes (392 ID)

The second embodiment of this invention was a golf ball with an icosahedron dimple pattern made from 392 dimples. The difference between this ball and the ball with the icosahedron dimple pattern made from 362 dimples was that there was one extra row of 30 dimples in the equatorial region. This resulted in the formation of one great circle at the equator (seam) that did not intersect any dimples. There were five different sizes of dimples labeled A through E in this golf ball.

Figure 5.3 shows the polar and equatorial regions for the icosahedron golf ball with 392 dimples and 5 different sizes.

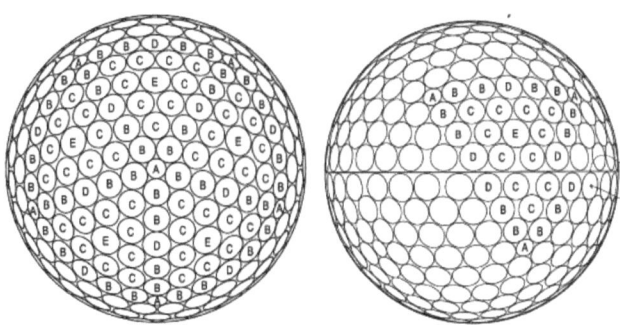

Figure 5.3 Polar (left) and equatorial (right) regions, Icosahedron with 392 dimples, five sizes[1]

The preferred dimple sizes for the icosahedron ball with 392 dimples are shown in Figure 5.4 (Table 2 in reference 7). I count 12 dimples labeled A, 125 dimples labeled B, 190 dimples labeled C, 45 dimples labeled D, and 20 dimples labeled E. I calculate that this ball with 392 dimples has 82.1 % surface coverage.

TABLE 2	
Dimple	Diameter (inches)
A	.11
B	.15
C	.155
D	.16
E	.17

Figure 5.4 Dimple sizes for Icosahedron with 392 dimples[1]

Examination of the equatorial region of the golf ball with the icosahedron dimple pattern consisting of 392 dimples in five different sizes shows that this ball is not a completely regular icosahedron, but is rather a skewed icosahedron. The 392 D dimple pattern became very popular and appeared on a number of Titleist and Pinnacle golf balls (see below).

Octahedron, 440 dimples, 6 sizes

A third embodiment of this invention was a golf ball that contained 440 dimples arranged in an octahedron pattern. The octahedron was made up of dimples arranged in eight spherical triangular regions that each contained 55 dimples. One of the spherical triangular regions is shown in Figure 5.5

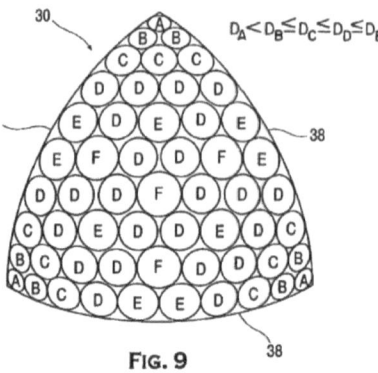

Figure 5.5 One of eight triangular faces of golf ball with 440 dimples, octahedron pattern[1]

There were six different sizes of dimples, labeled A-F. I count there are 24 dimples labeled A, 48 dimples labeled B, 72 dimples labeled B, 192 dimples labeled D, 72 dimples labeled E, and 32 dimples labeled F. My calculation[3] indicates that percent coverage is 82.3%

Dimple	Diameter (inches)
A	.09
B	.11
C	.14
D	.15
E	.16
F	.17

Figure 5.6 Dimple sizes for octahedron with 440 dimples, 6 sizes[1]

I do not have any golf balls in my collection that have the 440 O dimple pattern.

Aerodynamic Testing

The 392 dimple pattern that contained dimples of five different sizes (392 D) was chosen as the new golf ball dimple design by Acushnet through aerodynamic measurements using ballistic light screen technology, discussed below. Previously, the performance of the golf ball dimple patterns was measured by striking golf balls with a dual pendulum machine and then determining the carry distance and the carry plus roll distance by measuring them by hand. This procedure was expensive, time consuming, and not very precise. It needed many measurements in order to show the desired statistical confidence.

Starting in 2004, Laurent C. Bissonnette et al. obtained several patents[4-7] that disclosed the direct measurement of golf ball aerodynamic characteristics as opposed to measuring golf ball landing positions to determine the performance of the golf ball.

When a golf ball is struck, the dimples on the ball create a thin turbulent boundary layer around the ball. The turbulence energizes the boundary layer and aids in maintaining attachment to and around the ball to reduce the area of the wake (the turbulent flow area behind the ball with low pressure). When there is sufficient turbulence, the pressure behind the ball is increased and the drag is substantially reduced. Drag is defined as the force component parallel to the ball flight direction. Figure 5.7 shows the air flow around a golf ball in flight. The boundary layer forms at the stagnation point of the ball. B then grows and separates from the ball at points S1 and S2. Due to the backspin, the top of the ball moves in the direction of the airflow, which retards the separation of the boundary layer. The bottom of the ball moves against the direction of airflow, thus advancing the separation of the boundary layer at the bottom of the ball; therefore, the position of separation of the boundary layer at the top of the ball, S1, is further back than the position of separation of the boundary layer at the bottom of the ball, S2. This asymmetrical separation creates an arch in the flow pattern, requiring the air over the top of the ball to move faster and, thus, have lower pressure than the air underneath the ball. This causes lift, which is the upward force perpendicular to the flight path.

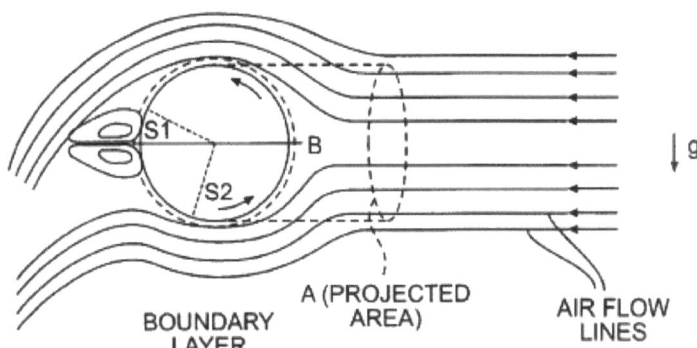

Figure 5.7 Air flow on a golf ball in flight[4]

Figure 5.8 below shows the forces acting on a golf ball in flight wherein $F_{Aerodynamic}$ = the total force on the ball, F_{Lift} = the lift force, F_{Drag} = the drag force, and $F_{Gravity}$ = the force of gravity. When struck by a golf club, the ball will fly to the right with a given velocity and will spin in the direction of the arrow at a given spin rate.

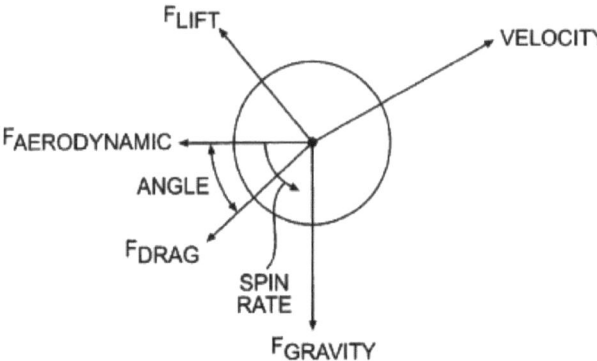

Figure 5.8 Forces operating on a golf ball in flight[4]

Aerodynamic testing of golf balls was carried out by measuring the lift (C_L) and drag (C_D) coefficients for a golf ball in flight for a given range of velocities and spin rates using an indoor test range with ballistic light screen technology.[8] This technique includes launching the ball along a flight path, measuring the velocity at two positions along the flight path, and then using the measured velocities to determine the coefficients of lift and drag. Measuring the velocity includes taking two images of the ball at the two positions where the time interval between images at each position is less than about 0.01 seconds. The ball launching area is capable of independently controlling the initial velocity, spin rate, and direction of the golf ball flight. The test range is equipped with high speed cameras, strobe lights, reflective panels, and so on, necessary to make the desired measurements. The golf balls are labeled with six reflective dots, the location of which the system uses to calculate the golf ball's spin rate, velocity, and direction.

The lift and drag coefficients are used to quantify the force imparted to a ball in flight and are dependent on air density, viscosity, ball speed, and spin rate. The influence of all these parameters may be captured by two dimensionless parameters Spin Ratio (SR) and Reynolds Number (N_{Re}). Spin Ratio is the rotational surface speed of the ball divided by the ball velocity. Reynolds Number quantifies the ratio of inertial to viscous forces acting on the golf ball moving through air and is equal to the ball diameter, times the ball velocity, times the air density, divided by the absolute viscosity of air.

The result of all this is that improved golf ball flight distance can be defined by two novel parameters that account for both lift and drag simultaneously. These are the magnitude of aerodynamic force (C_{mag}) and the direction of the aerodynamic force (Angle). The aerodynamic criteria for the golf balls of this invention are presented in Figure 5.9, which defines the magnitude of aerodynamic force (C_{mag}) and the direction of the aerodynamic force (Angle) as a function of the Reynolds number (N_{Re}) and the spin ratio (SR).

		Magnitude[1]			Angle[2] (°)		
N_{Re}	SR	Low	Median	High	Low	Median	High
230000	0.085	0.24	0.265	0.27	31	33	35
207000	0.095	0.25	0.271	0.28	34	36	38
184000	0.106	0.26	0.280	0.29	35	38	39
161000	0.122	0.27	0.291	0.30	37	40	42
138000	0.142	0.29	0.311	0.32	38	41	43
115000	0.170	0.32	0.344	0.35	40	42	44
92000	0.213	0.36	0.390	0.40	41	43	45
69000	0.284	0.40	0.440	0.45	40	42	44

AERODYNAMIC CHARACTERISTICS BALL
DIAMETER = 1.68 INCHES, BALL WEIGHT = 1.62 OUNCES

Figure 5.9 Aerodynamic Criteria for golf ball with improved flight distance[4]

What does this all mean? Well, think of the Reynolds number as being a measure of the velocity of the golf ball in air at normal temperature and pressure. For a golf ball that is 1.68 inch in diameter and weighs 1.62 ounces[9] and under ambient air density and viscosity, a Reynolds number of 230000 and SR of 0.085 describes a golf ball traveling at about 175 mph (struck by a driver) and a Reynolds number of 69000 and SR of 0.284 describes a ball traveling at about 50 mph (struck by a wedge). Figure 9 covers the entire range of expected golf ball velocities and trajectories. The spin ratio (SR) and the Reynolds number are dependent on one another. For each SR and N_{Re} in Figure 5.9, I calculate a golf ball rotation of about 3000 rpm[10]. This is a reasonable golf ball rotation rate for an average golf ball in flight.

The 'Magnitude' and the 'Angle' of aerodynamic force values in Figure 5.9 define the golf balls of this invention in the same way as the number of dimples, the dimple pattern, the percent coverage, or any other characteristic definition of a golf ball that may have been used before. In Figure 5.9 the patented golf balls (for a Reynolds number of 230000 and SR of 0.085), have a Magnitude of between 0.24 (Low) and 0.27 (High) with the preferred Magnitude of 0.265 (Median), and an Angle of between 31 (Low) and 35 (High) with a preferred Angle of 33 (Median). It is important to emphasize that the golf balls of this invention are defined by the aerodynamic performance given in this table and not by any other characteristic of the golf ball.

Golf Ball Symmetry

For a long time, golf ball manufacturers had known that the parting line or seam at the equator of the golf ball would influence the overall symmetry of the golf ball. Bissonnette et al. measured the lift and drag coefficients of a prior art golf ball (Titleist Professional with 392 IC dimple pattern) and a 392 ID golf ball of this invention. They used two different orientations of the golf balls. The first orientation was called the PH orientation (poles horizontal) and the other the PP orientation (pole over pole), in order to measure whether the golf balls gave the same characteristics regardless of the way they were oriented. This was done to determine whether the golf balls obeyed the USGA symmetry rule, which states a golf ball must act as if it had spherical symmetry. This was the first time that golf ball symmetry was determined with the necessary precision. The result of this study showed that the Titleist Professional golf ball (392 IC dimple pattern) had a 3.6 to 10.9% deviation in the aerodynamics between the PP and the PH orientations. This showed that the prior art Professional golf ball was not symmetric.

The testing also showed that the values of C_{mag} and Angle for the Titleist Professional were outside the preferred range for the C_{mag} and Angle in the Table of Figure 5.9, which defined the golf ball of this invention (392 ID dimple pattern).

In contrast, the golf ball with 392 dimples arranged in five different sizes (392 ID) had only 0.2 to 2.5% deviation between the PP and the PH orientations. This result indicated that this ball (392 ID) was more spherically symmetric than the prior art ball (392 IC). This golf ball had C_{mag} and Angle values within the preferred values for this invention.

Golf ball flight distances were also measured the old fashion way (by determining the distance traveled) for the Titleist Professional (392 IC) and a golf ball with the 392 ID dimple pattern. These results showed that the Titleist Professional golf ball did not travel as far as the new 392 ID golf ball in either the PP or PH orientation at two different golf ball speeds (168.4 mph speed or 145.4 mph speed).

Staggered Wave (SW) Parting Line Technology

Acushnet Company also took steps to minimize the seam or parting line in order to further improve the symmetry of golf balls. They developed technology[11] for molding a cover on a golf ball that would provide a non-planar parting line at the equator of the golf ball which improved overall golf ball symmetry. This non-planar parting line technology was called staggered wave (SW) technology, and golf balls with an offset seam appeared on several Titleist golf balls with the 392 ID dimple pattern. Figure 5.10 shows the non-planar staggered wave parting line (darker line) located at the equator of the golf ball.

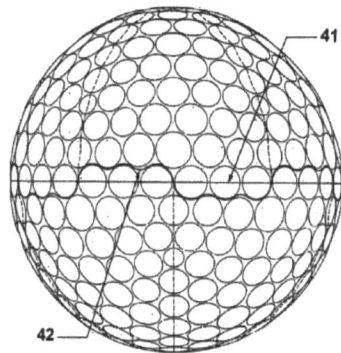

Figure 5.10 Golf Ball with Staggered Wave Seam Technology[11]

Golf Ball Construction

A variety of golf ball sizes and weights, constructions, and materials could be used to fit the aerodynamic characteristics shown in Figure 5.9. One way of adjusting the Magnitude and Angle to fit the aerodynamic criteria is through the use of different dimple patterns. The dimples could be spherical depressions, square mesh patterns, raised ridges and/or brambles. The preferred dimple patterns were: icosahedron, 360 dimples, five sizes, isosahedron 392 dimples, five sizes, and octahedron 440 dimples, six sizes.

The dimple profile could also be varied to fit the aerodynamic criteria of Figure 5.9. Dimples could have a spherical profile, a saucer-shaped profile[12], or a profile that was defined by edge radius and edge angle[13]. A new way to define and manufacture the dimple profile for golf balls of this invention was by the revolution of a catenary curve about an axis[14,15]. A parameter called the shape factor was an independent way to alter the volume ratio of a dimple while holding the dimple depth and radius fixed for a dimple defined by a catenary curve. Variation in the shape factor effectively changed the volume ratio of the dimple for a given depth, as shown in Figure 5.11. This is discussed in more detail in Chapter 6.

VOLUME RATIO AS A FUNCTION OF RADIUS AND DEPTH	
SHAPE FACTOR	VOLUME RATIO
20	0.51
40	0.55
60	0.60
80	0.64
100	0.69

Figure 5.11 Shape Factor and Volume ratio for dimple 0.05 inch radius, and 0.025 inch depth[14]

It was not necessary that every dimple be defined by a catenary curve. Some dimple profiles could be defined by a catenary curve and others could be circular. Nor was it necessary that every dimple have the same shape factor. A preferred golf ball was one that has at least 10% of the dimple defined by a catenary curve. A dimple with a profile defined by a catenary curve with a shape factor of less than about 40 had a smaller dimple volume than a dimple with a spherical profile. This resulted in a larger aerodynamic force angle and a higher trajectory. A dimple whose profile had a shape factor greater than 40 had a larger dimple volume than a spherical dimple. This resulted in a smaller angle of the aerodynamic force and a lower trajectory.

Golf balls of the present invention could be made of any type of ball construction. This included: one-piece design, two-piece design, three-piece design, a double core, a double cover, or multi-core and multi-cover construction. Different materials could be used. For example the cover could be made of a thermoset or thermoplastic, castable or non-castable polyurethane and polyurea, an ionomer resin, or balata. The golf balls could have solid, wound, liquid filled cores, dual cores, and multi-layer intermediate components.

Here are the Titleist golf balls in my collection that have the dimple pattern with 392 dimples arranged in the 392 ID dimple pattern. Those numbers marked with SW indicate that the golf balls had the staggered wave non-planar parting line technology.

Photographs of Titleist Golf Balls with 392 ID Dimple Pattern
Titleist DT Golf Balls (392 ID)

Figure 5.12 DT golf balls #168 (left) and #38 SW (right)

Figure 5.13 DT golf balls #114 (left), #11 (center), #88 SW (right)

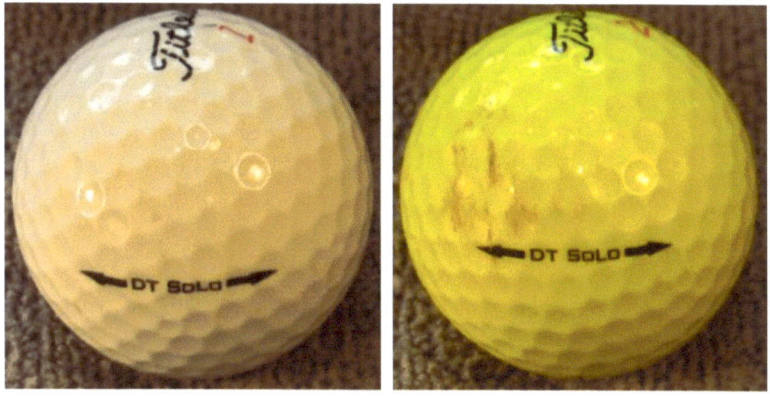

Figure 5.14 DT golf balls #91 SW (left) and #165 SW (right)

Titleist Tour Golf Balls (392 ID)

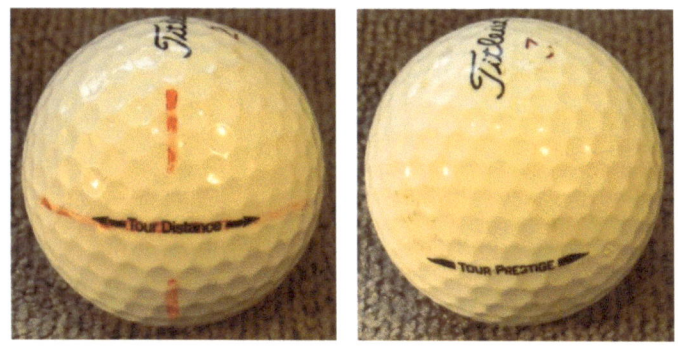

Figure 5.15 Tour Distance golf ball #127 SW (left) and Tour Prestige ball #63 (right)

Titleist HVC Golf Balls (392 ID)

Figure 5.16 HVC-Soft Feel # 140 (left) and HVC Tour SF #89 (right)

Titleist NXT Golf Balls (392 ID)

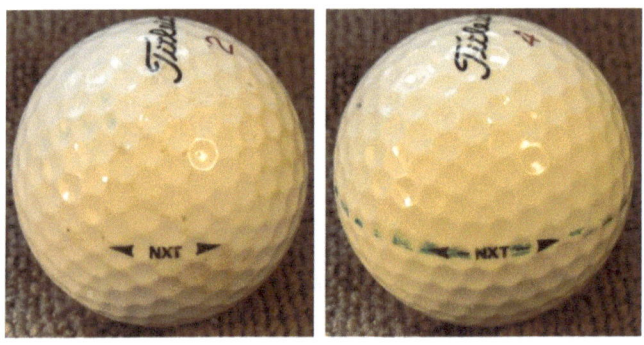

Figure 5.17 NXT golf balls #14 (left) and #155 (right)

Figure 5.18 NXT Tour golf balls #128 (left), #142 (center), and #158 SW (right)

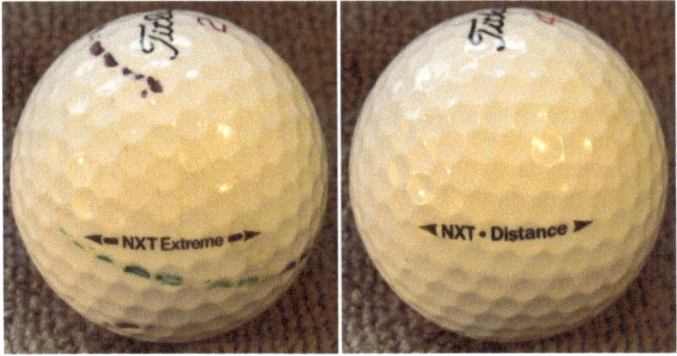

Figure 5.19 NXT Extreme golf ball #157 SW (left) and NXT Distance #126 (right)

Titleist HP3 Control Golf Ball (392 ID)

Figure 5.20 HP3 Control golf ball #87

Titleist Pro V1 Golf Balls (392 ID)

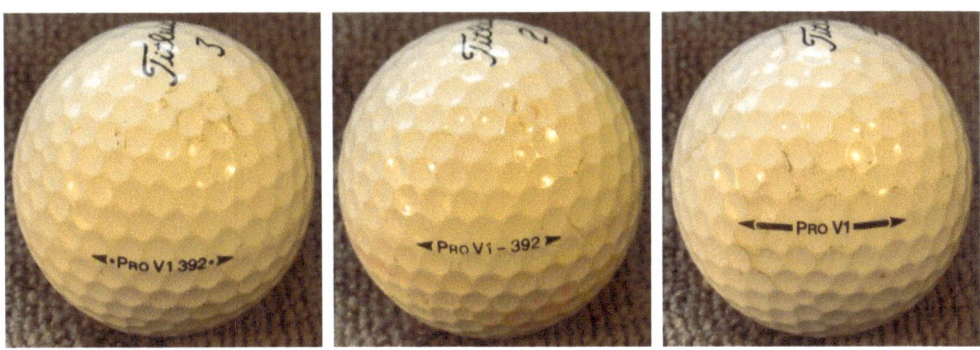

Figure 5.21 Pro V1 392 golf balls #43 (left), #41 (center), and #124 SW (right)

Figure 5.22 Titleist Pro V1 #44 SW

Pinnacle golf balls with the 392 D dimple pattern
Pinnacle Golf Balls with the Flag pin logo[16] (1985-2002)

Figure 5.23 Pinnacle golf balls #74 (left), #73 (center), and #101 (right)

Figure 5.24 Pinnacle golf balls #103 (left), #117 (center), and #149 (right)

Pinnacle Golf Balls with the Airfoil logo[17] (2002-2007)

Figure 5.25 Pinnacle golf balls #107 (left) and #108 (right)

Figure 5.26 Pinnacle Gold golf balls #109 (left) and #110 (right)

Figure 5.27 Pinnacle Exception golf ball #133 (left) and Pinnacle CLR golf ball #177[18] (right)

Pinnacle Golf Balls with the Airfoil Jet logo[19] (2007-2013)

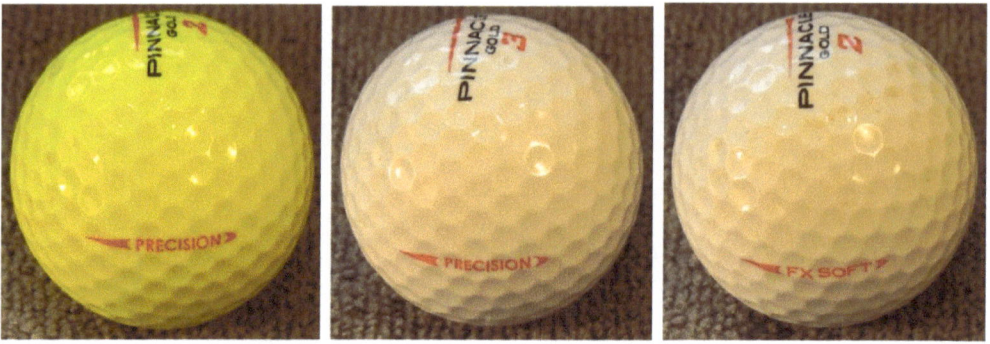

Figure 5.28 Pinnacle Gold golf balls #186 (left), #187 (center), and #105 (right)

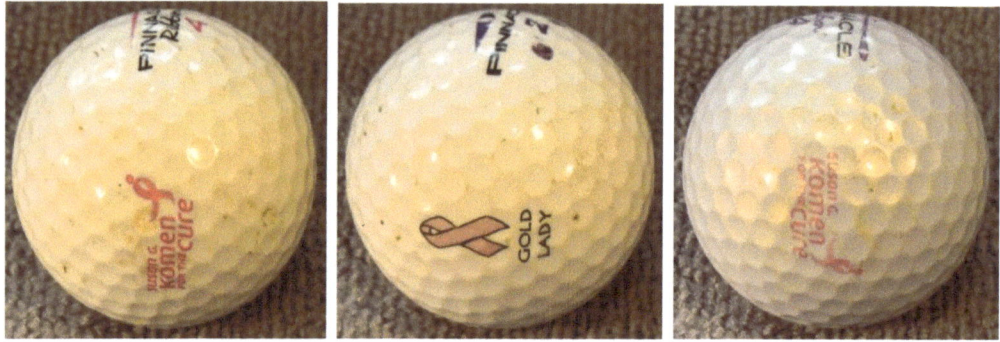

Figure 5.29 Pinnacle Ribbon golf balls #104 (left), #182 (center), and #183 (right)

Synopsis Chapter Five

- A new dimple pattern was introduced that had 392 dimples in five sizes (392 ID).
- This ball had greater than 80 % surface coverage, which results in better flight distance only if the dimples are a reasonable size (>0.10 inch)
- Aerodynamic testing using ballistic light screen technology was used to design the new dimple pattern.
- Dimples create a thin turbulent boundary layer around the surface of the ball resulting in decreased drag and increased lift.
- Golf ball flight symmetry was measured for the first time in two orientations, pole over pole (PP) and poles horizontal (PH).
- The Titleist Profession golf ball (392 IC), which had older dimple technology, did not have symmetric flight performance.
- A parting line at the seam of the golf ball affects the flight symmetry.
- Staggered wave parting line technology was introduced to improve the flight symmetry.

Chapter Six
Dimple Patterns for High Swing Speeds (252 I, 332 IE)
Priority Date 2003

Starting in 2003, Steven Aoyama and Douglas E. Jones obtained patent protection[1-6] for golf balls that had improved aerodynamic characteristics that yielded improved flight performance and longer ball flight. These patents taught that a golfer could control the initial golf ball speed, the launch angle, and the spin rate by using a particular club, but the distance a ball traveled depended on the ball aerodynamics, construction and materials, terrain, and weather. Previous improvements in golf ball design had resulted in a golf ball that had 392 dimples in two-five sizes and covered about 80% of the ball's surface. This golf ball was used by casual recreational golfers up to highly skilled professionals; however, professional golfers generally had a higher swing speed than the average player and there was no teaching in the art for a golf ball that was optimal for the very high ball speeds generated by today's professional players. These patents met that need.

The new dimple patterns for a golf ball that traveled further for a golfer who had high swing speeds were 1) 332 dimples, seven sizes, 84.2 % surface coverage, and 2) 252 dimples, six sizes, 84.9 % surface coverage. These dimple patterns are shown below.

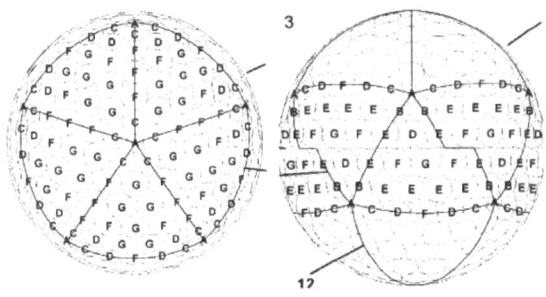

Figure 6.1 Polar region (left) and equatorial region (right) 332 IE dimple pattern[2]

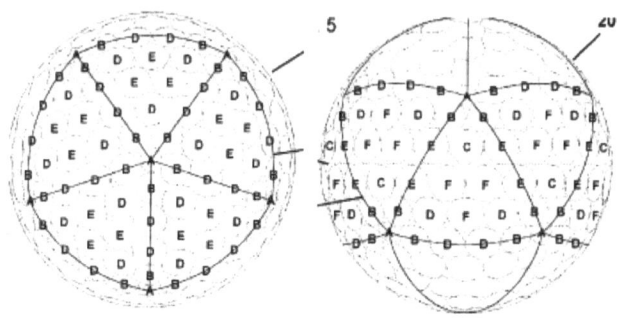

Figure 6.2 Polar region (left) and equatorial region (right) 252 I dimple pattern[2]

The dimple diameters and percent surface coverage are shown in Figure 6.3

Dimple	Diameter (inch)	Number of Dimples	Surface Coverage %
A	0.115	12	1.4
B	0.155	20	4.3
C	0.160	40	9.1
D	0.165	50	12.1
E	0.170	60	15.4
F	0.175	80	21.8
G	0.180	70	20.1
Total		332	84.2%

Figure 6.3 Dimple diameter and percent coverage for 332 IE dimple pattern[2]

Dimple	Diameter (inch)	Number of Dimples	Surface Coverage %
A	0.130	12	1.8
B	0.180	60	17.3
V	0.195	10	3.4
D	0.200	90	32.0
E	0.205	50	18.7
F	0.210	30	11.8
Total		252	84.9%

Figure 6.4 Dimple diameter and percent coverage for 252 I dimple pattern[2]

Any dimple shape, any golf ball construction, and any construction materials could be used for this new golf ball.

A preferred golf ball construction[7,8] for the golf ball with 332 dimples in seven sizes (332 IE) was a four-piece golf ball with an inner core, an outer core, an inner cover, and an outer cover. This construction was more useful than the three-piece golf ball with a core, an inner cover and an outer cover (Pro V1 golf ball), because the multiple layers of the four-piece golf ball (Pro V1x) made it possible to easily modify the moment of inertia (MOI) of the golf ball. The MOI was one of the factors that determined the spin rate of the ball. For example, if the center of the golf ball has high density, the MOI is low and the ball will spin more rapidly than if the perimeter of the golf ball has high MOI. The density of the layers can be modified by the addition of high density fillers to the different layers during the molding cycle.

The preferred inner core of this golf ball was prepared by mixing together cispolybutadiene base rubber, a zinc diacrylate crosslinking agent, a free radical initiator, a filler (density modifier), and a cis-trans isomerization catalyst; placing the mixture into the golf ball mold; and then adding heat. This produced a polybutadiene core that was soft (low compression) but had high resilience (CoR). An outer core layer was then molded over the inner core. The achieved goal was a golf ball that had a soft inner core, a harder outer core, an inner cover that was harder than the outer core, and finally an outer cover that was softer than the inner cover. The inner cover consisted of a hard Surlyn ionomer material while the soft outer cover layer was a thin thermoset polyurethane material.

The dimple volume was an important variable for this invention. It was preferred that the golf balls have a relatively large total dimple volume. The dimple volume could be varied by changing the edge angle of the dimple if the dimples were circular or by changing the shape factor if the dimples were defined by a catenary curve.

A dimple formed using a catenary curve with a shape factor less than about 40 will have a smaller dimple volume than a dimple with a spherical profile. A shape factor greater than about 40 will result in a larger dimple volume.

Volume Ratio as a Function of Radius and Depth	
SHAPE FACTOR	VOLUME RATIO
20	0.51
40	0.55
60	0.60
80	0.64
100	0.69

Figure 6.5 Volume Ratio and Shape Factor[10]

Figure 6.6 shows the shape of the catenary curve as the shape factor varies from about 20 to about 100 wherein 'a' is the shape factor,' r' is the radius of the dimple, 'd' is the depth of the dimple, and 'vr' is the volume ratio of the dimple.

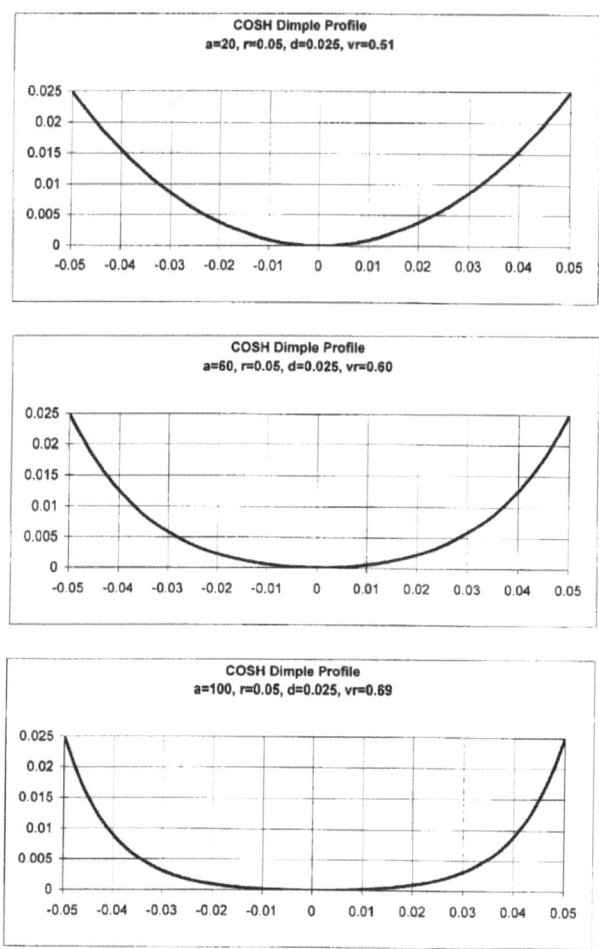

Figure 6.6 Catenary curve as a function of the shape factor[10]

It was discovered that a golf ball that had high total dimple volume would produce a low trajectory flight and a golf ball that had low total dimple volume would produce a high trajectory flight. Thus, changing the shape factor for dimples defined by a catenary curve was a way to change the aerodynamic characteristics of a golf ball without changing the overall dimple pattern. It was not necessary that catenary curves be used on every dimple on a golf ball. Nor was it necessary that every dimple had the same shape factor on the same ball. Therefore once a dimple pattern for the golf ball was selected, alternate shape factors could be tested in the ballistic light gate test range to empirically determine the catenary shape factor that provided the desired aerodynamic characteristics.

Aerodynamic Criteria

The aerodynamic criteria claimed in these patents were the magnitude of the aerodynamic force (C_{mag}) and the direction of the aerodynamic force (Angle) for the range of golf ball velocities and spin rates that encompassed the flight parameters for typical golf ball trajectories. Spin Ratio (SR) and Reynolds Number (N_{RE}) were used to capture all the factors that would influence golf ball flight. Measurement of the lift coefficients (C_L) and the drag coefficients (C_D) was carried out by using ballistic light screen technology as discussed in Chapter 5.

Five different golf ball prototypes of this invention with different total dimple volumes were prepared and distance tested against commercially available golf balls. All of the prototypes contained 332 dimples in seven sizes. The prototype golf balls had high total dimple volumes that were at least about 1.50% of the volume of the ball. The distance testing showed that the prototype golf balls of this invention traveled farther than Pinnacle Gold Distance, Titleist Pro V1, Callaway CTU Red, and Callaway HX Red golf balls when struck at very high impact speeds to produce initial velocities of 175-178 mph. At slower initial velocities of 158-160 mph, the prototype golf balls traveled distances that were comparable to the distance traveled by the commercially available golf balls.

The high total dimple volume golf balls that contained 332 dimples in seven sizes were found to have relatively low lift and low drag coefficients (C_L and C_D) at high velocities (N_{Re}= 180,000 and SR=0.110 for example during the golf ball ascent), and relatively high lift and high drag coefficients at low velocities (N_{Re}=70,000 and SR=0.188 for example during the golf ball descent). This is purported to mean that such a golf ball would have lower lift during the ascent so the ball travels further and may have more roll. Furthermore, the golf ball would have higher lift during the descent, and thus maximize the carry distance.

Titleist Golf Balls that have the 332 IE Dimple Pattern
Titleist Pro V1x Golf Balls (332 IE)

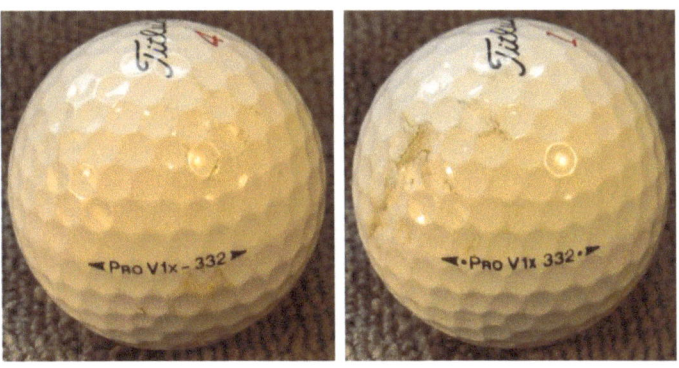

Figure 6.7 Titleist Pro V1 golf balls #20 (left) and #50 (right)

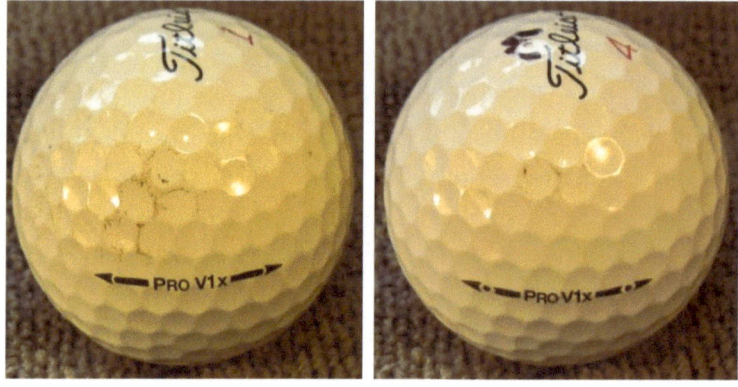

Figure 6.8 Titleist Pro V1 golf balls #55 (left) and #137 (right)

Titleist NXT Golf Balls (332 IE)

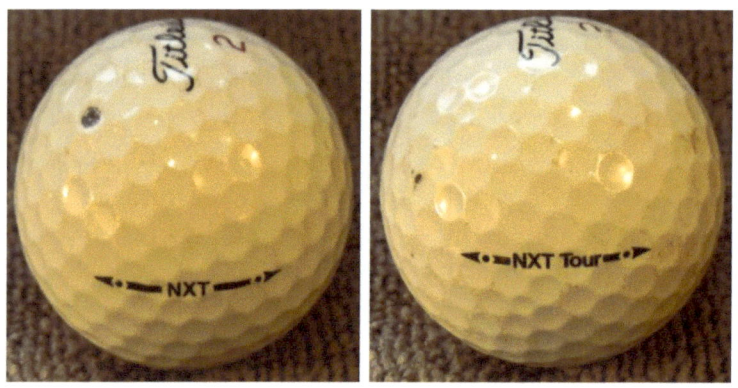

Figure 6.9 Titleist NXT golf ball #156 (left) and NXT Tour golf ball #125 (right)

Titleist Tour Distance and Titleist Velocity (332 IE)

Figure 6.10 Titleist Tour Distance golf ball #163 (left) and Titleist Velocity #170 (right)

Titleist Golf Ball with the 252 I Dimple Pattern
Titleist DT Carry Golf Ball (252 I)

Figure 6.11 Titleist DT Carry golf ball #79

The Titleist DT Carry golf ball has 252 dimples arranged in an icosahedron dimple pattern (252 IR). There are fewer and larger dimples in this golf ball than there are in the golf ball with 332 dimples (332 IE). The dimple pattern for the DT Carry golf ball is a completely regular icosahedron because the equatorial region does not contain a row of dimples at the equator or seam of the golf ball.

Pinnacle Golf Balls with the 332 IE Dimple Pattern

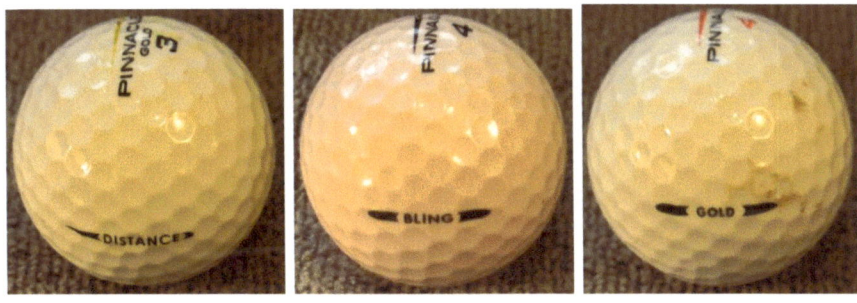

Figure 6.12 Pinnacle golf balls #148 (left), #185 (center), and #118 (right)

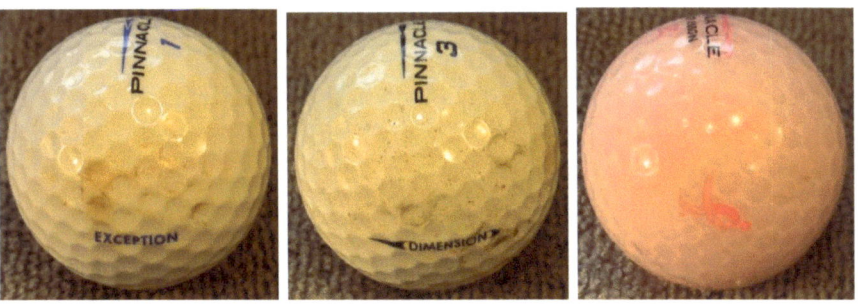

Figure 6.13 Pinnacle golf balls #119 (left) #121 (center), and #184[9] (right)

Figure 6.14 Pinnacle golf balls #176 (left) #179 (center) and #120 (right)

Figure 6.15 Pinnacle golf ball #78 (left) and #188 (right)

Synopsis Chapter Six

- Two new dimple pattern 332 dimples seven sizes (332 IE) and 252 dimples six sizes (252 I) were developed.
- These new patterns had high surface coverage and high dimple volume.
- High dimple volume leads to low trajectory flight and low dimple volume leads to high trajectory flight.
- At least 10% of dimples were designed using a catenary curve profile.
- A golf ball that has high moment of inertia (MOI) leads to low spin and one with low MOI leads to high spin.
- The new 332 IE ball of this invention had low coefficient of lift (C_L) at high velocity (ascent) and high C_L at low velocity (descent) resulting in long distance at high swing speeds.

Chapter Seven
Symmetric Dimple Patterns (302 CO, 328 T, 342 CO, 352 T, 376 T, 330 IE*)
Priority Date 2008

In 2009, Aoyama and Nardacci et al. filed a patent[1] for a golf ball with improved symmetry. This patent taught that improvements in the aerodynamics of golf ball design made in the past did not always result in a golf ball that obeyed the USGA rule on symmetry. This rule stated that a ball must fly the same distance and for the same time regardless of how it was oriented. The asymmetry was often the result of parting lines or great circle paths that were formed as a result of the golf ball dimple pattern, or as a result of the seam at the equator normally formed during manufacturing of the ball.

Titleist developed a new process[2] for forming dimple patterns on the surface of a golf ball that eliminated parting lines or great circle paths on the surface of the ball. This resulted in a golf ball with improved overall spherical symmetry.

This process consisted of the following steps: first, generate a domain from a polyhedron and choose control points to further generate one or more irregular domains based on the control points; second, pack the irregular domains with dimples; and finally, tessellate the irregular domain to cover the surface of the golf ball. The control points could consist of the center (C) of the polyhedron face, a vertex (V) of the polyhedron, a midpoint (M) on an edge of the polyhedron, among others. The patent provided several methods for generating the irregular domains based on the set of control points. They are defined as follows:

1. Center to midpoint (C→M);
2. Center to center (C→C);
3. Center to vertex (C→V);

4. Midpoint to midpoint (M→M);
5. Midpoint to vertex (M→V); and
6. Vertex to vertex (V→V).

This was demonstrated for the octahedral dimple pattern with 360 dimples using method 4, the midpoint to midpoint method.[3]

Figure 7.1 showed how to draw an irregular domain (14a) on one triangular face of a spherical octahedron on the surface of a golf ball. Line segments (18) were drawn from one midpoint (M_1, M_2, and M_3) of each edge (E_1, E_2, and E_3) to another edge of the triangular region. There were a total of eight irregular domains (14a) on the surface of the golf ball, one on each of the eight faces on the surface of a spherical octahedron.

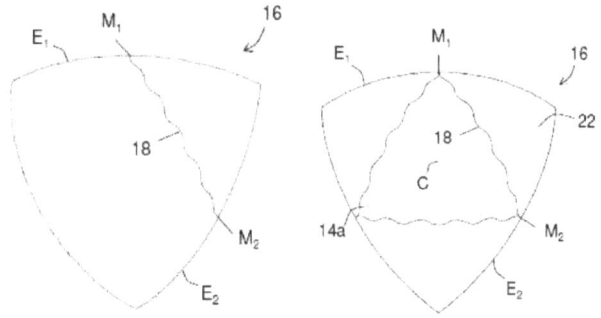

Figure 7.1 Irregular domain (14a) on one triangular face of an octahedron[3]

The element (22) which is bound by the line segment (18) and one half of a edge (E_1) and one half of edge E_2) at the respective midpoints (M_1 and M_2) defined one quarter of a second irregular domain (14b) shown in Figure 7.2. There were a total of six-second irregular domains (14b) on the surface of the golf ball, one for each vertex of a spherical octahedron.

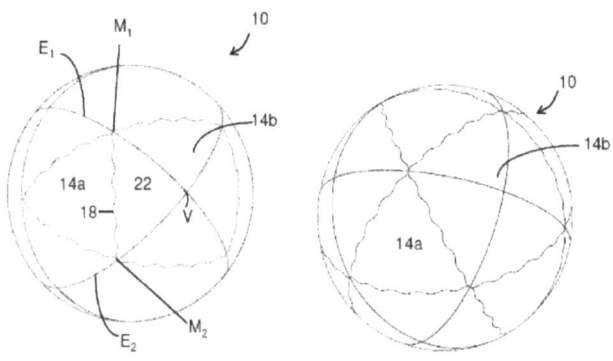

Figure 7.2 Irregular domains 14a and 14b on surface of golf ball[3]

The irregular domains were then filled with dimples as shown in Figure 7.3. Domain 14a contained a total of 15 dimples and domain 14b contained a total of 40 dimples. Over the entire surface of the golf ball, there were 120 dimples in the eight triangular shaped domains (14a) and 240 dimples in the six square shaped domains (14b) for a total of 360 dimples.

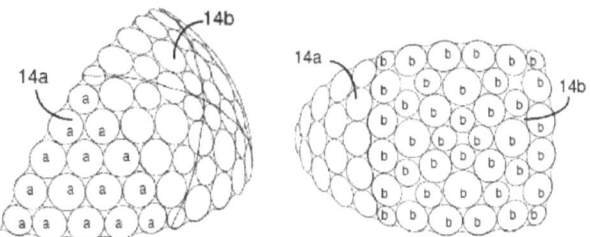

Figure 7.3 Irregular domains filled in with dimples[3]

The dimple pattern made from the eight triangular shaped domains (14a) and the six square shaped domains (14b) for the octahedral golf ball with 360 dimples is shown in Figure 7.4.

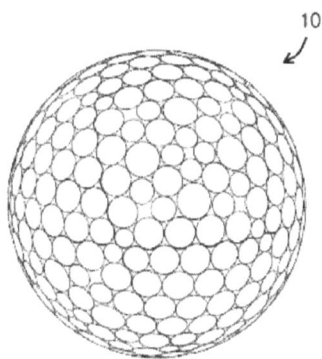

Figure 7.4 Dimple pattern for octahedral pattern with 360 dimples[3]

When the irregular domains are patterned onto the surface of a golf ball as discussed above, the symmetry of the underlying polyhedron is preserved while minimizing or eliminating great circles due to parting lines. Figure 7.5 shows the symmetry order as a function of the type of polyhedron chosen.[4] These high orders of symmetry may result in more even dimple distribution, higher packing efficiency and improved means to mask the ball parting line on the surface of the golf ball resulting in higher symmetry.

Symmetry of Golf Ball of the Present Invention as a Function of Polyhedron		
Type of Polyhedron	Type of Symmetry	Symmetrical Order
Tetrahedron	Chiral Tetrahedral Symmetry	12
Cube	Chiral Octahedral Symmetry	24
Octahedron	Chiral Octshodial Symmetry	24
Dodecahedron	Chiral Icosahedial Symmetry	60
Icosahedron	Chiral Icosahedial Symmetry	60

Figure 7.5 Symmetry as a function of the polyhedron type[3]

Seamless Parting Line (SL) Technology

Seamless parting line technology (SL) was developed based on a superposition of a base waveform and a secondary waveform using computer aided design (CAD) technology.[5-8] The base waveform was dependent on the symmetry of the dimple pattern. For example, a tetrahedral dimple pattern would have a wavelength 1/3 of the circumference of the mold cavity; an octahedral dimple pattern, a wavelength 1/4 the circumference of the mold cavity; and an icosahedral dimple pattern, a wavelength 1/5 the circumference of the mold cavity. The secondary waveform was machined to follow the profile of the equator dimples, thereby not crossing any of the equator dimple perimeters. This produced the wavy or corrugated parting line at the equator. Figure 7.6 shows the non planar parting line created for a golf ball consisting of both a base waveform and a secondary waveform.

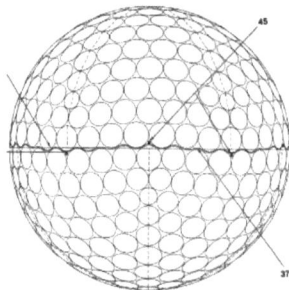

Figure 7.6 Seamless parting line for a golf ball[6]

Tessellated Dimple Patterns

Here are the golf balls I have in my collection that contain the novel tessellated dimple patterns with the seamless parting line at the seam described above. The first pattern is based on a tetrahedron, which consists of four triangular regions on the surface of a sphere. Figure 7.7 shows an orthographic representation of a tetrahedron on the surface of a sphere.

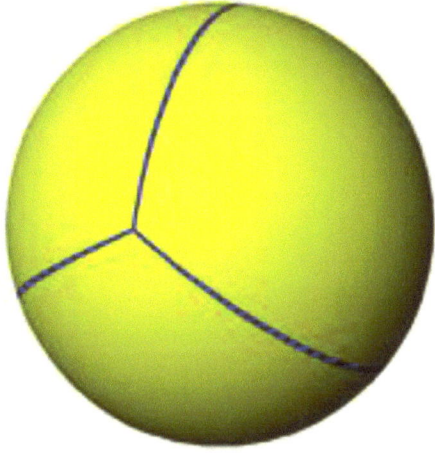

Figure 7.7 Orthographic representation of a tetrahedron[9]

Titleist Pro V1 and AVX Golf Balls (352 T)

The Titleist Pro V1 and the Titleist AVX golf balls have the 352 T dimple pattern. This dimple pattern consists of 88 dimples of various sizes arranged in four triangular regions on the surface of a sphere. Figure 7.8 shows the top view (polar view) of the 352 T dimple pattern.

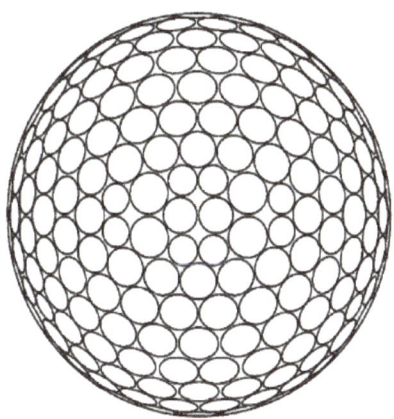

Figure 7.8 The 352 T dimple pattern[10] (top view)

Photographs of Golf Balls with the 352 T Dimple Pattern

Figure 7.9 Balls #45 (left), #151 (center), and #46 (right)

Figure 7.10 Balls #64 (left), #152 (center), and #226 (right)

Titleist Pro V1x and Velocity Golf Balls (328 T)

The Titleist Pro V1x and the Titleist Velocity golf balls have the 328 T dimple pattern. This dimple pattern consists of 82 dimples of various sizes arranged in four triangular regions on the surface of a sphere. Figure 7.11 shows the top view of the 328 T dimple pattern.

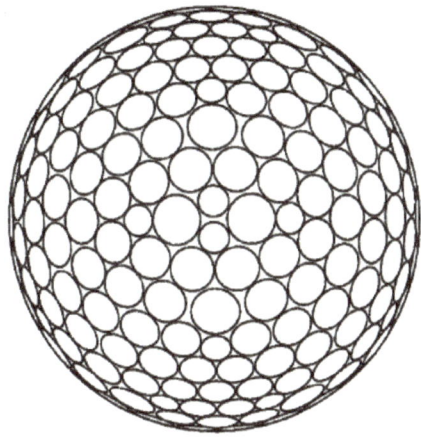

Figure 7.11 The 328 T dimple pattern[11] (top view)

Photographs of Titleist Golf Balls with the 328 T Dimple Pattern

Figure 7.12 #147 (left) and #56 (right)

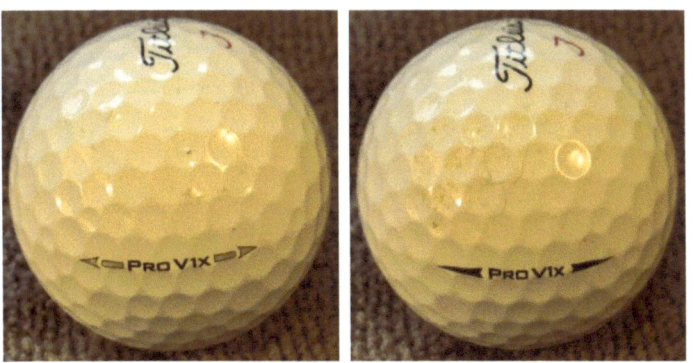

Figure 7.13 Balls #57 (left) and #227 (right)

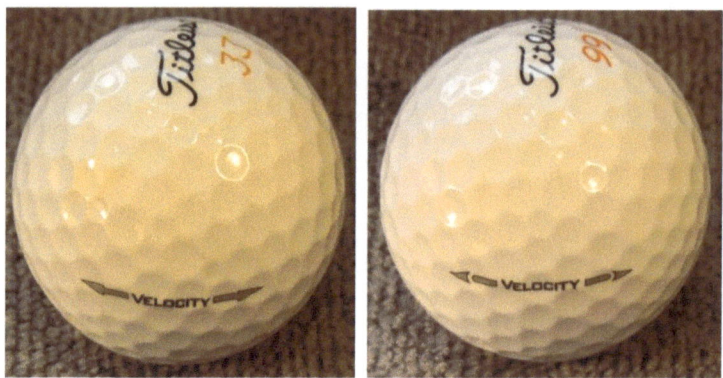

Figure 7.14 Balls #22 (left) and #98 (right)

Titleist DT Trusoft and DT Solo Golf Balls (376 T)

The Titleist DT Trusoft, and DT Solo golf balls have the 376 T dimple pattern. This dimple pattern consists of 94 dimples of various sizes arranged in four triangular regions on the surface of a sphere. Figure 7.15 shows the top view of the 376 T dimple pattern.

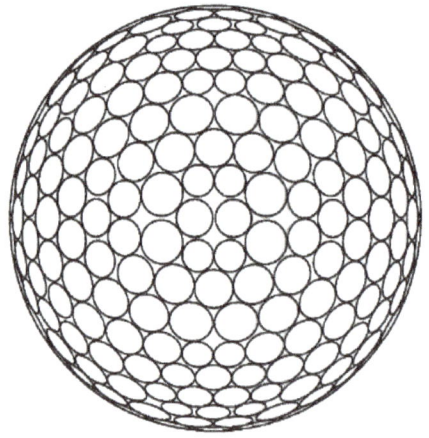

Figure 7.15 The 376 T dimple pattern[12] (top view)

Photographs of Titleist Golf Balls with the 376 T Dimple Pattern

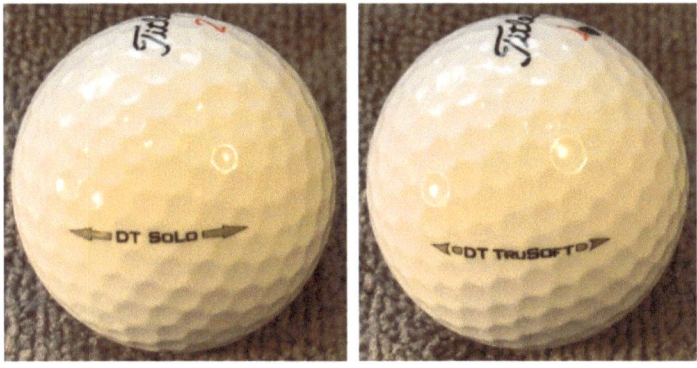

Figure 7.16 Balls #53 (left) and #62 (right)

Titleist NXT Tour and NXT Tour S Golf Balls (302 CO)

The Titleist NXT Tour and the NXT Tour S golf balls have the 302 CO dimple pattern. This is a cuboctahedron dimple pattern with a total of 302 dimples. This dimple pattern consists of six square regions that have 33 dimples and eight triangular regions that have 13 dimples arranged on the surface of a sphere. Figure 7.17 shows an orthographic representation of a cuboctahedron on the surface of a sphere.

Figure 7.17 Orthographic representation of a cuboctahedron[13]

Photographs of Titleist Golf Balls with the 302 CO Dimple Pattern

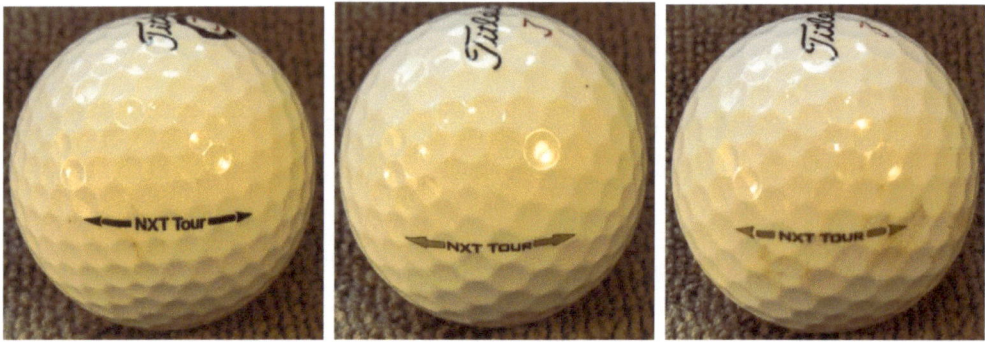

Figure 7.18 Balls #158 (left), #59 (center), and #159 (right)

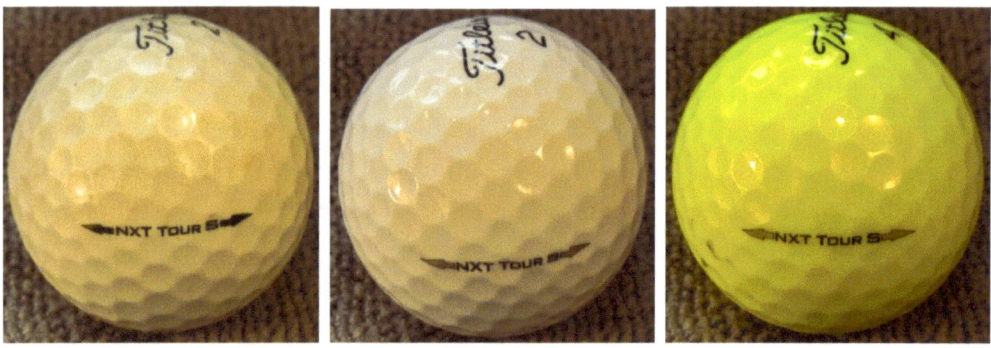

Figure 7.19 Balls #150 (left), #60 (center), and #61 (right)

Titleist Tour Soft Golf Ball (342 CO)

The Titleist Tour Soft golf ball has the 342 CO dimple pattern. This is a cuboctahedron dimple pattern with a total of 342 dimples. This dimple pattern consists of six square regions that have 37 dimples and eight triangular regions that have 15 dimples arranged on the surface of a sphere. Both the 302 CO and the 342 CO dimple patterns are really extensions of the cuboctahedron dimple pattern discussed in Chapter 4. These dimple patterns are spherically symmetrical. Figure 7.20 shows the top view of the 342 CO dimple pattern.

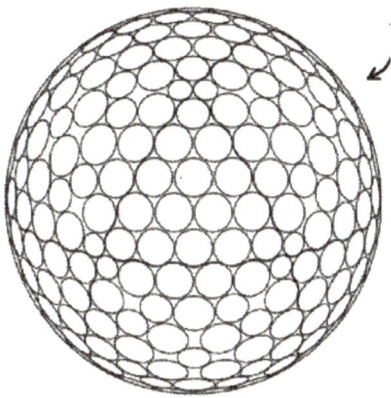

Figure 7.20 The 342 CO dimple pattern[13] (top view)

Photograph of the Titleist Golf Ball with the 342 CO Dimple Pattern

Figure 7.21 Ball # 248

Modified Dimple Technology (M)

Additional modification to the surface of the golf ball to improve spherical symmetry was described in two patents by Madson et al.[14,15] The edge angle, diameter, or depth of the dimples were modified to improve the spherical symmetry. The dimples to be modified were chosen from the set of gray/black dimples shown in Figure 7.22. This figures show the 332 IE dimple pattern as viewed from the pole of the golf ball. The process of discovering how to determine the position of the modified dimples, and how many dimples to modify was carried out by using the ballistic light screen technology discussed in Chapter 5.

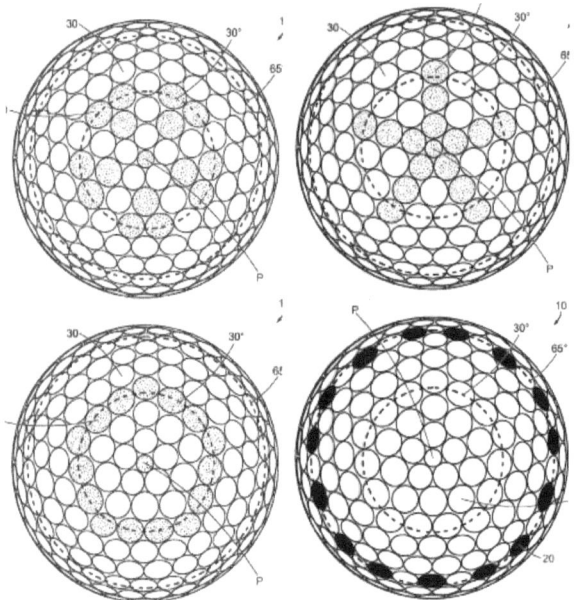

Figure 7.22 Polar view of modified dimples[1]

The dimple modifications consisted of changing the edge angle, diameter, or depth of the dimples. It is very difficult to determine whether the edge angle, diameter, or depth of the dimples have changed by a visual inspection of the golf ball; however it is likely that a golf ball made after 2011 that has the 332 IE dimple pattern has modified dimples. The Titleist and Pinnacle golf balls that meet this criteria are: Titleist Velocity (ball #170, Figure 6.10), Pinnacle Gold (ball #118, Figure 6.12), Pinnacle Gold (ball #179, Figure 6.14), Pinnacle Gold Ribbon (ball #184, Figure 6.13), and Pinnacle Bling (ball #185, Figure 6.12).

Another option was to remove some dimples entirely. As it turns out, there are three golf balls in my golf ball collection that have some dimples removed entirely, as shown in Figure 7.23. These three golf balls had one dimple removed from each of the two poles of the golf ball that had the 332 IE dimple pattern. These golf balls have a total of 330 dimples arranged in the 330 IE* dimple pattern. They are the Titleist Gran Z (ball #169), Pinnacle Long Drive (ball #111), and Pinnacle gold <<FX Long (ball # 123).

Photographs of Golf Balls with the 330 IE* Dimple Pattern

Figure 7.23 Balls #169 (left), #111 (center), and #123 (right)

Synopsis for Chapter Seven

- The USGA rule on symmetry says that a golf ball must fly the same distance and for the same time regardless of how it is oriented.
- Acushnet developed an improved process forming symmetric dimple patterns on the surface of golf balls.
- The new dimple patterns that were developed were 352 T, 328 T, 376 T, 302 CO, and 342 CO.
- Seamless parting line technology using computer aided design (CAD) was patented.
- Improved symmetry also resulted on golf balls by modifying some of the dimples on the golf balls that had the 332 IE dimple pattern.
- In some cases dimples were removed entirely to improve the symmetry dimple pattern 330 IE*.

Chapter Eight
Reduced Distance Golf Balls
Priority Date 2005

The USGA and the Royal and Ancient Golf Club of St. Andrews (R&A) are responsible for setting the rules for golf balls. Appendix III – The Ball, which can be found in the USGA rules[1] contains the specification for golf ball weight, size, spherical symmetry, initial velocity, and overall distance standard. These are:

1. The ball must not be substantially different from the traditional and customary form and make.
2. A ball must not weigh more than 1.620 ounces (45.93 gm).
3. A ball must have a diameter of not less than 1.680 inches (42.67 mm).
4. A ball is designed and manufactured to behave symmetrically.
5. The golf ball must meet the initial velocity specification (< 250 ft/s plus 5 ft/s maximum tolerance).
6. The golf ball must meet the overall distance (carry and roll) standard (< 317.0 yards plus 3 yards maximum tolerance).

All golf ball manufacturers may submit golf balls to the USGA and the R&A for testing. If the balls conform to the rules they are entered onto the Conforming Golf Ball List. The USGA publishes the Conforming Golf Ball List every month. The USGA List contains useful information for every golfer, including the golf ball's pole/seam marking, color, construction, spin rating, number of dimples, country, and manufacturer. Only golf balls that appear on the USGA list can be used by golfers who play in USGA and PGA tournaments.

When the USGA revised the Overall Distance and Symmetry Test, which set the test requirements for maximum overall distance for a golf ball, this presented a problem for Acushnet Company and other golf ball manufacturers because some golf balls traveled farther than the 320 yards maximum allowed. This was because over the years the scientists and engineers at Acushnet and other companies had researched and improved the aerodynamics of golf ball flight, and had optimized the golf ball construction and materials to such an extent, that the golf balls were traveling too far and did not conform to the new USGA rule. It was an important problem that needed to be solved because only USGA approved golf balls could be used in tournament play.

Acushnet started addressing this problem in 2005,[2] when the USGA instituted a research project to design and make a prototype golf ball that would reduce the maximum ball distance by 15 or 25 yards. Their goal was to achieve a golf ball that flew shorter than the current performance balls while maintaining the appearance of a high performance trajectory without adversely affecting the balls durability, spin, and feel.

In 2005-2012 Sullivan et al. obtained a number of patents[3-6] for golf balls that would travel a reduced distance. These patents were directed to designing and making a high performance golf ball having reduced distance while maintaining a high performance trajectory. This was accomplish by a combination of: lowering the coefficient of restitution (CoR) of the golf ball, thickening the cover, reducing the golf ball weight, increasing the golf ball diameter, lowering the dimple percent surface coverage, decreasing the diameter of the dimples, increasing the dimple edge angle, and increasing the coefficient of drag and the coefficient of lift, so that the distance traveled was reduced by 15-25 yards.

The Sullivan invention reduced the CoR from a value of about 0.800 to about 0.600-0.780. The CoR (resiliency) is the ratio of the velocity of a golf ball after it is impacted by a surface (such as the face of a golf club), divided by the velocity prior to impact. The CoR can vary from 0 to 1.0. A CoR of 1.0 is a perfectly elastic collision, and a CoR of 0 is a perfectly inelastic collision (does not bounce back). The substitution of low resilient (low CoR) elastomers such as butyl rubber, halogenated butyl rubber, polyisobutylene, or other polymers for some of the polybutadiene in the core was one way to reduce the CoR of a golf ball. This had an added benefit in that substituting low resilient elastomers for some of the polybutadiene in the core often resulted in an increase in the softness of the golf ball.

Compression is a measure of how much a golf ball deforms when struck by an object such as a golf club. A person with a high swing speed would compress or deform a golf ball to a larger extent than a person with a low swing speed and the golf ball would have high velocity and travel a long distance. A person with a low swing speed would prefer a golf ball with low compression because it would take less force to compress the ball and the ball would feel softer; however, don't confuse compression (softness) with resiliency (CoR). A golf ball could have a high CoR (high resiliency) and feel hard (like the early two-piece golf balls like the Titleist HVC), or high resiliency and feel soft very soft (like the Titleist Pro V1, which I discuss later). The difference depends on the chemistry of the materials that make up the golf ball core.

In order to produce a golf ball that didn't travel as far, the weight of the golf ball could also be reduced from a normal value of 1.62 ounces to a value preferably of about 1.45 to 1.58 ounces. In addition the diameter of the golf ball could be increased from a value of 1.68 inches to a value preferably of about 1.695 to 1.725 inches. These two changes did not violate any USGA rules because the USGA rule for the weight and size of a golf ball states that the ball should not weigh more than 1.62 ounces, nor be less than 1.68 inches in diameter.

An example of a reduced distance golf ball reported in the Sullivan patents was one that had an icosahedron dimple pattern (332 IE) with 332 dimples in seven sizes. This dimple pattern was first described in Chapter 6 for a golf ball with improved distance; however, for a golf ball with reduced distance, the dimple diameter and percent surface coverage were modified compared to the ball described in Chapter 6. The new reduced distance golf ball could also contain dimples that had a high edge angle (18 - 22°) compared to the golf balls described in Chapter 5. This would result in a ball that had higher turbulence and thus a higher drag coefficient than the golf balls in Chapter 6, resulting in decreased distance.

The dimple diameter and percent surface coverage for the reduced distance golf ball and the golf ball from Chapter 6 are shown in Figures 8.1 and 8.2. The golf ball dimple percent surface coverage was only 70.0% for the reduced distance golf ball, which can be compared to the golf ball reported in Chapter 6 that had 84.2 % surface coverage. The dimple diameters for the golf ball with reduced distance were also smaller than those for the golf ball in Chapter 6.

	Dimples and Dimple Pattern		
Dimple	Diameter (inch)	Number of Dimples	Surface Coverage %
A	.105	12	1.2
B	.141	20	3.5
C	.146	40	7.6
D	.150	50	10.0
E	.155	60	12.8
F	.160	80	18.2
G	.164	70	16.7
Total		332	70.0%

Figure 8.1 Dimple diameters and percent coverage for reduced distance golf ball[3]

Dimples and Dimple Pattern of the First Embodiment

Dimple	Diameter (inch)	Number of Dimples	Surface Coverage %
A	0.135	12	1.4
B	0.155	20	4.3
C	0.160	40	9.1
D	0.165	50	12.1
E	0.170	60	15.4
F	0.175	80	21.8
G	0.180	70	20.1
Total		332	84.2%

Figure 8.2 Dimple diameters and percent coverage for golf ball from Chapter 6, Figure 6.3

The changes that were necessary to produce the golf balls of this invention were determined by measuring the aerodynamic performance of golf ball prototypes using a ballistic light screen technology. Reduced distance golf balls prepared according to this invention had a relatively high coefficient of drag $C_D > 0.26$ @ N_{Re} 150,000 and a spin rate of 3000 rpm, and $C_D > 0.29$ @ N_{Re} 120,000 and a spin rate of 3000 rpm. The coefficient of lift was also high: $C_L > 0.21$ @ NRe 150,000 and 3000 rpm and greater than 0.23 at NRe 120,000 and 3000 rpm.

The reduced flight distance golf ball of this invention retained the appearance of a normal trajectory. This is shown in Figure 8.3, which shows the trajectories of a Pro V1 golf ball (normal weight, CoR of 0.810), a minimum weight ball (CoR of 0.700), and a minimum weight ball (CoR of 0.650). In all cases, the trajectory was the same at the beginning of flight and only the total flight distance varied.

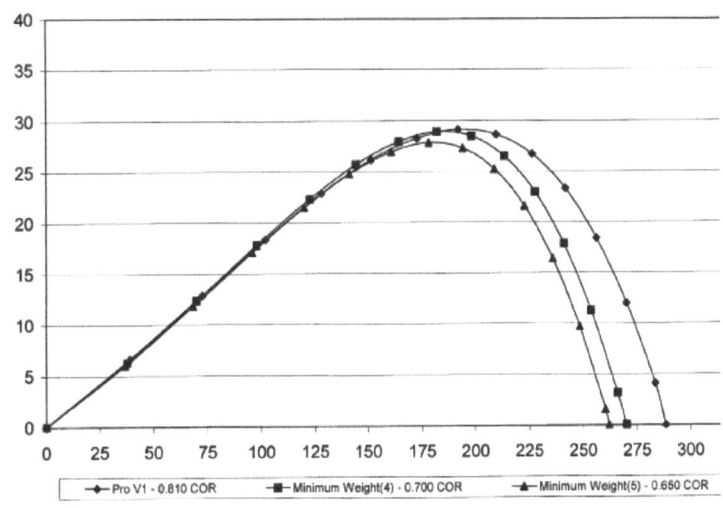

Figure 8.3 Trajectories of Pro V1 ball and two minimum weight golf balls[3]

How can you tell if you're using a golf ball that has reduced distance and a high performance trajectory so you don't violate the 2011 USGA distance rule? This seems like a difficult question to answer because it is very difficult for the average person to determine the C_D, C_L, the CoR, the compression, the dimple size and edge angle of the dimples, or the composition of the core, or cover material of a golf ball; however, there are three things that you can do. First, you can measure the diameter of the golf ball to see if the diameter is increased compared to the USGA standard of 1.68 inches. There are no golf balls in my collection made after 2011 that have reduced distance because of an increased diameter. The golf ball diameter data that I have measured for the golf balls in my collection is reported in the tables in the second part of this book.

Second, you can weigh the golf ball and determine if the weight of the golf ball is reduced compared to the USGA standard of 1.62 oz. There are three golf balls in my collection made after 2011 that have reduced weight in order to meet the USGA distance standard. They are two Titleist Velocity golf balls (ball # 170, Figure 6.10, and ball #22, Figure 7.14), and Pinnacle Gold (ball # 179, Figure 6.14).

Third, if the golf ball does not have reduced weight or an increased diameter, and is on the USGA conforming list after 2011, then the resiliency (CoR), the percent dimple coverage, the dimple diameter, or the dimple edge angle has been modified so the golf ball will have reduced distance and conform to the USGA distance rule. I think it is safe to say that every Titleist and Pinnacle golf ball made after 2011 has been modified in some way so it doesn't violate the USGA distance rule.

It was a little bit disturbing for me to learn that Acushnet Company had to modify the golf balls they produced so they would not travel too far. I get an enormous amount of satisfaction from striking a golf ball and seeing it travel a long distance, especially when it is also on line to the target. Perhaps Titleist golf balls had to be modified to a greater extent than golf balls from other manufacturers by these regulations, because the Titleist website[7] contains a presentation entitled "Tradition & Technology – Preserving the Balance" that discusses this very issue of golf ball regulations.

The Titleist presentation summarizes the changes made in the sport of golf starting in the 1950s and proceeding to the present day. The presentation identifies six contributing variables to the increase in distance today compared to the 1950s:

1. The development of the low spin, solid core golf ball
2. The introduction of the oversize driver and graphite shaft technology
3. Improved golf course agronomy and lower grass height in the fairways
4. Improvements and innovations in golf swing technique and instruction

5. Development of new technology such as launch monitors
6. Bigger and stronger golfers can generate higher swing speed

Titleist presented evidence that showed there was a strong correlation of driving distance to club head size, lower grass height in the fairways (inverse correlation) and player fitness. The low spin solid core golf ball had only a small correlation to driving distance. Nonetheless, the playing field has been leveled and all golf balls must now travel the same distance. One consolation is that because Titleist golf balls may incorporate low resilient (low CoR) elastomers for some of the polybutadiene in the core of a golf ball, these golf balls will have lower compression, feel very soft, and still travel as far as the USGA allows

Synopsis for Chapter Eight

- In 2011 the USGA limited the distance that a golf ball could travel to 320 yards under the USGA overall distance (carry and roll) standard.
- As a result, Acushnet Company designed a new golf ball that would travel 15-25 yards less while maintaining a high performance trajectory.
- Acushnet Company lowered the CoR, the percent surface coverage, and the weight of the golf ball, and increased the dimple diameter to meet this objective.

Chapter Nine
Low Swing Speeds
Priority Date 2006

In Chapter 6, I talked about the golf ball technology that was developed for players with very high swing speeds. But what about players with low swing speeds? For many years golf balls were produced for golfers with low swing speeds. These golf balls had lower compression (80 compression) than golf balls for players with average swing speeds (90 compression), and high swing speeds (100). The low compression golf balls usually had the seam label printed in red to indicate low compression.

In 1999, Morgan et al. filed a patent[1] for a low drag and weight golf ball designed for the low swing speed golfer. Professional golfers typically have high swing speeds, which are often greater than about 120 mph. An average golfer generally has swing speeds in the range of about 70 to 95 mph. A low swing speed golfer has a swing speed that is less than 70 mph. Do you know your swing speed? The most reliable way to determine your swing speed is to go to your local golf shop and get a club fitting. They use a launch monitor to determine it. A cheaper but less reliable way is to hit some golf balls at a driving range with your driver and determine the average carry distance (do not count roll distance). You may need a friend to stand at a place where they can easily determine where the ball lands. The distance in yards is then divided by 2.3 to give you the swing speed in mph. For example, if your drive carries 230 yards, then your swing speed is 100 mph.

When a player strikes a ball, a portion of the energy from the club head is transferred to the ball as ball speed, and another portion of the energy as ball spin. A golfer with a low swing speed often has insufficient energy for both high ball speed and spin. This means there is less energy to give the golf ball sufficient velocity and lift. This results in ballistic flight instead of aerodynamic flight.

The Morgan patent[1] helped overcome this problem by designing a golf ball with improved ballistic flight for golfers with a low swing speed. This patent taught that what was needed to accomplish this was to reduce the coefficient of drag, to reduce the weight of the golf ball, and to reduce the golf ball spin rate. The drag coefficient was reduced by using a golf ball dimple pattern that had high percent surface coverage. The preferred golf balls of this invention weighed less than 1.60 oz. The golf ball spin was reduced by using a ball with a hard cover and a soft core (low compression). The soft core was made by using CaO instead of ZnO as the filler in the core. Lower golf ball spin also resulted when shallow dimples were used. This was accomplished by using dimples with a low edge angle, which resulted in low volume dimples.

A golf ball with a large number of small dimples also gave lower spin than a golf ball with a small number of large dimples. The Morgan patent proposed two different dimple patterns—one with 642 dimples in a regular icosahedron pattern with two sizes of dimples, and 77% surface coverage, and a second dimple pattern with 440 dimples in an octahedral pattern with six sizes. The octahedral pattern had 82% surface coverage. The dimples had a low drag dimple shape, which included dimples that were relatively shallow with a low edge angle. This gave the golf ball a high lift coefficient, high spin, and a high trajectory; however, I do not have any golf balls in my collection that have these two dimple patterns. The Morgan patent was an important first step in understanding how to improve the golf ball for low swing speed golfers; however, there remained a need for a golf ball that was optimized for the golfer with a low swing speed.

From 2006-2013, Sullivan filed new patents[2-4] for golf balls designed for golfers with low swing speeds. They found there was an important relationship between a golf ball spin rate, moment of inertia (MOI), lift (C_L) and drag (C_D) coefficients that could be optimized for golfers with low swing speeds.

The dimple patterns used for these golf balls had relatively large numbers of dimples with high percent surface coverage (e.g., 362 dimples in five sizes arranged in an icosahedron dimple pattern, 392 dimples in five sizes arranged in an icosahedron dimple pattern, and 440 dimples in six sizes arranged in an octahedral dimple pattern).

They discovered two ways to provide a golf ball for golfers with low swing speed. Case 1 provided a golf ball with high lift ($C_L \geq 0.20$), low drag ($C_D \leq 0.22$) and low spin (about 3100 rpm at a ball speed of 120 mph). In order to produce a golf ball with high lift and low drag, they needed to design a golf ball with high percent surface coverage and shallow dimples. In order to produce a golf ball with low spin, they needed to add more weight to the perimeter of the ball which increased the moment of inertia (MOI ≥ 0.46 oz/in^2). A golf ball that was designed with a soft core, a hard cover, and a high coefficient of restitution (CoR) would aid in achieving a golf ball with high lift, low drag, and low spin. Sullivan found that a golf ball with this particular combination of high lift, low drag, and low spin (high MOI) was novel, useful, and not obvious, and they were able to obtain a U.S. patent for this invention. This is shown in Figure 9.1.

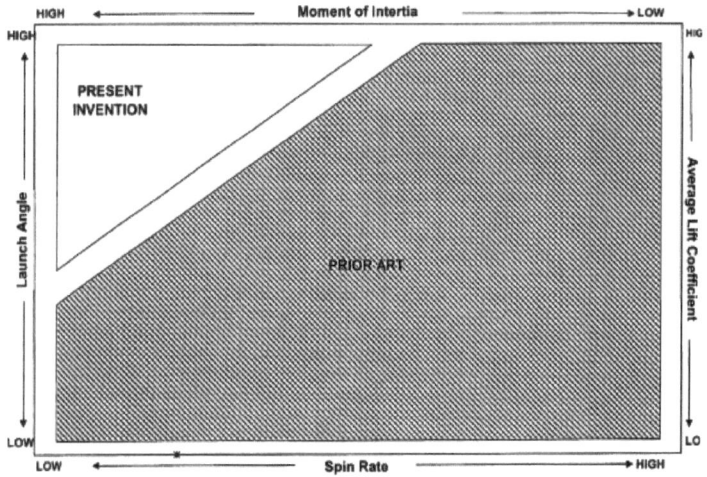

Figure 9.1 Golf Ball for a low swing speed golfer according to Case 1[3]

Needless to say, it is rather difficult to determine by visual inspection whether a golf ball has been designed to fit all the parameters for Case 1; however, some important factors to look for include: reduced weight (<1.60 oz.), an aerodynamic dimple pattern, and a ball with a low spin rating (L-L). I have identified three golf balls in my golf ball collection that potentially meet these criteria. They are PINNACLE γ GOLD LADY (ball #182, Figure 5.29), PINNACLE *Ribbon* (ball #183, Figure 5.29), and PINNACLE GOLD RIBBON (ball #184, Figure 6.13).

Case 2 provided a golf ball with low lift ($C_L < 0.20$), low drag ($C_D < 0.22$) and high spin (about 3700 rpm at a ball speed of 120 mph). In order to produce a golf ball with low lift and low drag, they needed to design a golf ball with high percent surface coverage and deep dimples. In order to produce a golf ball with high spin, they needed to add more weight to the center of the ball, which decreased the moment of inertia (MOI < 0.40 oz/in^2). A golf ball that was designed with a soft core, a soft cover, and a high coefficient of restitution (CoR) would aid in achieving low lift, low drag, and high spin. Sullivan found that a golf ball with this particular combination of low lift, low drag, and high spin (low MOI) was also novel, useful, and not obvious, and they were able to obtain a U.S. patent for this invention. This is shown in Figure 9.2.

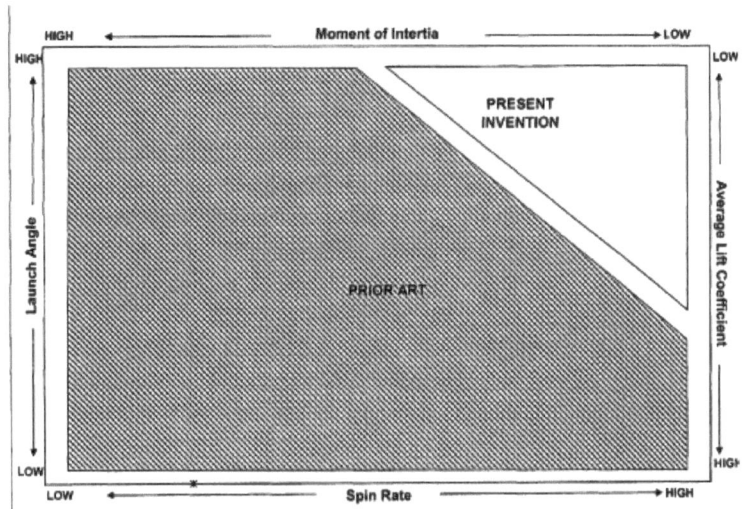

Figure 9.2 Golf Ball for a low swing speed golfer according to Case 2[3]

Some golf balls designed to fit Case 2 might include the parameters: reduced weight (<1.60 oz.), an aerodynamic dimple pattern, and a moderately high spin rating (L-M). I have identified four golf balls in my golf ball collection that potentially meet these criteria. They are Titleist DT SoLo golf balls (ball #91, Figure 5.14), (ball #165, Figure 5.14), (ball #53, Figure 7.16), and Titleist DT Trusoft (ball #62, Figure 7.16).

A multilayer golf ball is one that contains both a center and an outer core. This type of multilayer core construction is particularly suitable for adjusting the moment of inertia of a golf ball. The addition of high density (high specific gravity) materials to the center of a golf ball is one way to change the moment of inertia. If the center of the golf ball has a high specific gravity, the ball has a lower moment of inertia, and the ball will have higher spin. Likewise, if the outer core has a high specific gravity, the ball has a higher moment of inertia, and the ball will have lower spin. One way to remember how the moment of inertia affects the spin rate is by considering an ice skater that is doing a spin on the ice. When the ice skater's arms are outstretched, the spin rate is slow and when the skater's arms are close to his or her body, the spin rate increases.

The specific gravity of the golf ball center or outer core can also be adjusted by adding low density materials to the core or intermediate layers. Some examples of low density materials are foams with hollow sphere fillers or microspheres in a polymeric matrix, or polymers where nitrogen gas is whipped into at least one component of the polymer.

Synopsis Chapter Nine

- In the past, golf balls for low swing speed players had low compression and low weight.
- A low swing speed has insufficient energy for both high ball velocity and spin.
- Acushnet patented two golf ball designs for players with slow swing speeds.
- Case 1 was for a golf ball with high lift, low drag, and low spin.
- Case 2 was for a golf ball with high spin, low lift and low drag.
- The spin rate can be controlled by modifying the moment of inertia of the golf ball.
- Low spin results when the moment of inertia is high.
- High spin results when the moment of inertia is low.
- When a golf ball has deep dimples, low lift results.
- When a golf ball has shallow dimples, high lift results.

Chapter Ten
USGA Conforming Golf Ball List

The early chapters of this book have discussed different dimple patterns that appear on the surface of Titleist and Pinnacle golf balls. A person can easily determine the number of dimples and the dimple pattern on a golf ball by visual inspection. Well maybe that is an oversimplification because it does take some work to count the number of dimples and to determine which pattern is used on any given golf ball. But you get the idea. Dimple pattern identification is a sure fire way to determine the start date for the introduction of a golf ball because a new dimple pattern is almost always protected by a U.S. patent. The priority date of the patent then becomes the earliest date at which a particular golf ball with a particular dimple pattern was introduced. If a patent was filed before 1995, the term of a U.S. patent began at the issue date and continued for an additional 17 years. If a patent was filed after 1995, the term of a U.S. patent began at the filing date and continued for an additional 20 years[1].

Chapter	Dimple Pattern	Earliest US Patent No.	Priority Date	Issue Date	Expiration Date
1	336 A				
2	324 IA and 384 IB	4,729,861	20-Mar-72	8-Mar-88	2005
3	392 IC	4,804,189	24-Oct-83	14-Feb-89	2006
4	440 CO and 416 OQ	4,948,143	6-Jul-89	14-Aug-90	2007
5	392 ID	5,957,786	3-Sep-97	28-Sep-99	2117
6	252 I and 332 IE	6,916,255	6-Jan-03	12-Jul-05	2023
7	Symmetric dimple patterns	8,029,388	31-Oct-08	4-0ct-2011	2028
8	Reduced distance	7,481,723	29-Aug-05	27-Jan-09	2025
9	Low swing speed	8,617,003	18-Jan-06	31-Dec-13	2026

Figure 10.1 Patent Priority Dates for Acushnet Company Dimple Patterns

Starting in 1972, the USGA began publishing a list of all golf balls from all manufacturers that conform to the rules of golf. This list is called the USGA Conforming Golf Ball List. This list was first published in 1972[2] and today the list is updated and published once a month by the USGA[3]. Golf balls that are included on this list are those that do not violate any USGA rules and thus are permitted to be used in all PGA and USGA golf tournaments.

The information contained in the USGA conforming list is also useful for all golfers. The recreational golfer can use the information contained in the USGA conforming list to help golfers determine which golf ball they should be using. Important information can be obtained from the spin rating, which tells the spin rating of a golf ball when struck by a driver and when struck by a lofted iron. For golfers who are unable to control unintentional side spin, the best option might be to choose a golf ball that has low (L) spin rating instead of medium (M) or high (H) spin rating. For a golfer who can control side spin, another option is to choose a golf ball with either an M or H spin rating. For the professional golfer, the USGA conforming list determines which golf ball he or she can use in a USGA or PGA tournament.

The USGA Conforming Golf Ball List may also be used to find when a golf ball was first introduced. In principle, this can be done by finding the date when a particular pole/seam marking first appeared on the USGA list; however, there are difficulties using the USGA List to date golf balls. The problem is that originally the USGA List was only printed as a hard copy, and these older printed copies of the USGA List have been difficult to locate. In addition, more recent copies of the USGA List, which are published on the internet, are not regularly saved and archived. More often only the most recent USGA list can be found on line.

Sometimes the USGA lists for prior years can be found on the internet. I have obtained copies of the USGA conforming lists for the years 2005- 2018[4], and I have used the information contained in these lists to summarize what is known about many of the golf balls in my golf ball collection. Since the USGA lists are rather cumbersome to use, I have extracted the useful information for the golf balls made by Acushnet Company and put this information in a series of tables that appear in subsequent chapters of this book. These tables were created for the Titleist and Pinnacle golf ball pole/seam markings in my collection.

One of the difficulties in using the USGA lists is the way the seam markings are reported on the USGA list. For example, the seam marking for golf ball #64 in my collection, the 2015 Titleist Pro V1 golf ball, is reported in the USGA list as '**(arrow bar) Pro V1 (bar arrow) with (arrows & bars) in gray**'. I label this ball as ← **Pro V1 → (arrows in gray)** instead. Likewise the seam marking for golf ball #152, the 2017 Pro V1 golf ball is reported in the USGA list as '**(wedge) Pro V1 (wedge)**'. I label this ball as ≪ **Pro V1**≫. If the reader has any problem in identifying the seam marking on the golf ball, please refer to the actual photo of golf balls reported in the earlier chapters to see exactly what the seam marking looks like.

Wouldn't it be nice if the data in USGA Conforming Golf Ball data base could be archived in such a way that golfers could take a photo of the pole and seam marking for a golf ball that they just found, for example, and send it to an application on their mobile device and quickly determine whether the ball was a legal USGA golf ball and could be used during their round of golf? Or if golf ball collectors wanted to know, for example, the number of dimples, the ball construction, the spin rating or the date of introduction of a vintage golf ball that was made after 1972, to include in their golf ball collection? USGA, if you are listening, please create an application that will make this information available to golfers and golf ball collectors!

The next part of this book is arranged according to the pole/seam marking on the golf ball and not according to the dimple pattern on the golf ball. These chapters will discuss the construction, the spin rating, and other relevant information for the Titleist and Pinnacle golf ball pole/seam markings in the following order: Titleist Pro V1 Golf Balls (Chapter 11), Titleist Pro V1x Golf Balls (Chapter 12), Titleist NXT Golf Balls (Chapter 13), Titleist Tour Golf Balls (Chapter 14), Titleist DT Golf Balls (Chapter 15), Pinnacle Golf Balls (Chapter 16), and Vintage Golf Balls (Chapter 17). Finally in Summary & Conclusions (Chapter 18) I will summarize everything I've discussed so far, and will provide decision criteria for choosing what golf ball to use.

Synopsis Chapter Ten

- The USGA Conforming Golf Ball List is published online every month.
- The USGA list can be used by golfers to determine the spin rating of the golf ball that they are using.
- Archived USGA lists can be used by golf ball collectors to help date the introduction of golf ball models in the marketplace.

Chapter Eleven
Titleist Pro V1 Golf Balls

The next chapters are directed not to the dimple pattern on the surface of the golf ball, as discussed in the early chapters of this book, but rather to the different golf ball models (i.e., the name on the seam of the golf ball).

The Titleist Pro V1 Golf Ball

The first Titleist Pro V1 golf ball was introduced in 1999. This ball was a three-piece ball that contained a solid polybutadiene core, a hard ionomer inner cover and a thin soft polyurethane outer cover.[1] What made this ball special was that the polybutadiene core was softer than previous Titleist cores (for example the HVC core) but just as resilient (high CoR). The Pro V1 golf ball had two covers: an ionomer inner cover that was made of a hard high flexural modulus material (Surlyn), which gave the ball low spin and long distance, and a thin soft polyurethane cover, which gave the ball soft feel. This ball had the distance benefits of a two-piece ball with a hard cover when struck with a club like a driver, plus the high spin and feel characteristics of a traditional soft covered wound ball when struck with a club like a wedge. The patent for making the thin polyurethane cover on a golf ball was filed[2] in 1998. The steps included forming the golf ball core, injection molding an inner cover layer around the core, and casting an outer cover layer around the inner cover layer. Figure 11.1 shows a cross section of a golf ball (10) with a core (12), inner cover (16a), and outer cover (16).

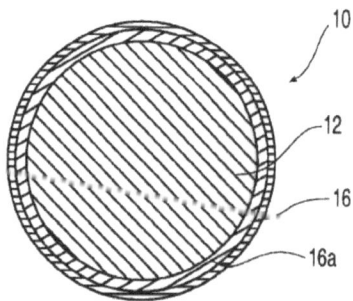

Figure 11.1 Cross section of a golf ball with a core, inner cover, and outer cover[11]

In 2007, Callaway Golf Company sued Acushnet Company claiming that the Pro V1 (and Pro V1x) golf balls infringed four Callaway U.S. patents that disclosed a thin and very soft polyurethane cover used as part of a solid-core multilayer golf ball.[3,4] Callaway Golf Company acquired the four patents when it purchased the Top Flite golf ball business from Spalding in 2003. Acushnet did not deny the allegations but asserted that the four Callaway U.S. patents were invalid. After an initial ruling in favor of Callaway Golf Company, Acushnet appealed and won a ruling that said the four Callaway patents were invalid because they were not novel.

It seems that every two years, Acushnet introduced a new version of their Pro V1 golf balls. The new versions probably included improvements that Acushnet was continuously making to their Pro V1 technology. They put a slightly different name on the seam of the golf ball in order to document this change. Figure 11.2 shows the changes that have taken place for the Titleist Pro V1 golf ball over the period 1999 to 2017. Figure 11.2 shows the page number in my golf ball notebook where the golf ball is listed, the label on the pole and the seam, the date of introduction of the golf ball,[5] the seam construction (staggered wave SW or seamless SL), the chapter in which a photo of the ball appears, the dimple pattern, the golf ball construction (3P, three-piece ball), the cover construction (2c, 2-covers), the spin rating (M-H, medium spin for the driver, high spin for a lofted club), the golf ball diameter, and the golf ball weight. This information is provided by the USGA in their Conforming Golf Ball List,[6] or the result of measurements that I made on these golf balls[7].

In 2003, the Pro V1 golf ball dimple pattern changed from 392 IC1 to 392 ID. This was because golf balls with the 392 ID dimple pattern traveled farther than those with the 392 IC1 dimple pattern (Chapter 5). In 2011, the Pro V1 golf ball dimple pattern changed once again from 392 ID to 352 T, because golf balls with the 352 T dimple pattern had improved spherical symmetry compared to those with the 392 ID pattern (Chapter 7). Because the USGA revised the overall distance rule in 2011, the Pro V1 that was introduced in 2011 must have included changes that were made to the dimple percent surface coverage, the dimple edge angle, and the chemical composition of the core (CoR) to limit the distance the golf ball would travel. As shown by my measurements (diameter and weight) of the Pro V1 golf balls, I did not see any significant changes in the size or the weight of the golf balls; nor did I see any change in the spin rating (M-H) of the golf balls over the period of 1999-2017 for the Pro V1 golf balls.

The spin rating of a golf ball can be an important factor for both the average player and for the professional golfer. The average player may prefer a golf ball that has a low spin rating so the effects of unintentional side spin (hooks and slices) may be minimized. The professional golfer may prefer a golf ball that has a high spin rating so his or her approach shots to the green can have backspin and stop

notebook number	pole label	seam label	date	chpt.	dimple pattern	BALL	CENTER	COVER	SPIN	diameter in.	weight oz.	seam	swing speed
18	Titleist 3	Pro V1 392	1999	3	392 IC1	3P	SC	2c	M-H	1.68			
42	Titleist 1	< Pro V1 ∘ 392 >	2001	3	392 IC1	3P	SC	2c	M-H	1.69			
43	Titleist 3	<∘ Pro V1 392 ∘ >	2003	5	392 ID	3P	SC	2c	M-H	1.68			
41	Titleist 2	< Pro V1-392 >	2005	5	392 ID	3P	SC	2c	M-H	1.68			
124	Titleist 4	<— Pro V1 —>	2007	5	392 ID	3P	SC	2c	M-H	1.67		SW	
44	Titleist 4	<∘ — Pro V1 — ∘ >	2009	5	392 ID	3P	SC	2c	M-H	1.69	1.62	SW	
45	Titleist 4	← Pro V1 →	2011	7	352 T	3P	SC	2c	M-H	1.69	1.61	SL	
151	Titleist 4	← Pro V1 →	2011	7	352 T	3P	SC	2c	M-H	1.67	1.62	SL	slow
46	Titleist 3	← Pro V1 → (arrows in gray)	2013	7	352 T	3P	SC	1c	M-H	1.69	1.61	SL	
64	Titleist 5	<—Pro V1 —> (arrows in gray)	2015	7	352 T	3P	SC	1c	M-H	1.69	1.61	SL	
152	Titleist 2	<< Pro V1 >>	2017	7	352 T	3P	SC	1c	M-H	1.67	1.61	SL	

Figure 11.2 Summary of Titleist Pro V1 Golf Balls from 1999 to the present

near the pin, and so they may intentionally draw or fade the golf ball around a tree or other object in direct line to the target. The Pro V1 golf ball had medium spin when struck by the driver and high spin when struck by a short iron. I think the lesson here is that only those players who are able to control unintentional side spin should chose to play a Pro V1 golf ball.

According to the information contained in the USGA conforming list, there was a change in the number of covers on the Pro V1 golf ball cover in 2013 from two covers to one. In order to find out why I decided to cut open several Pro V1 golf balls to determine visually what was going on. I found the 2013 Pro V1 golf ball still contained three layers: a core and what appeared to be two covers. I believe that after 2013 Titleist began calling the inner cover an intermediate layer instead, resulting in three layers: a core, an intermediate layer, and a cover. Surprisingly, I found that the color of the cores for the Pro V1 golf balls changed dramatically over the period of 1999 to 2017. Figure 11.3 shows photos of the different color cores for the Pro V1 golf balls over the period of 1999 to 2015.

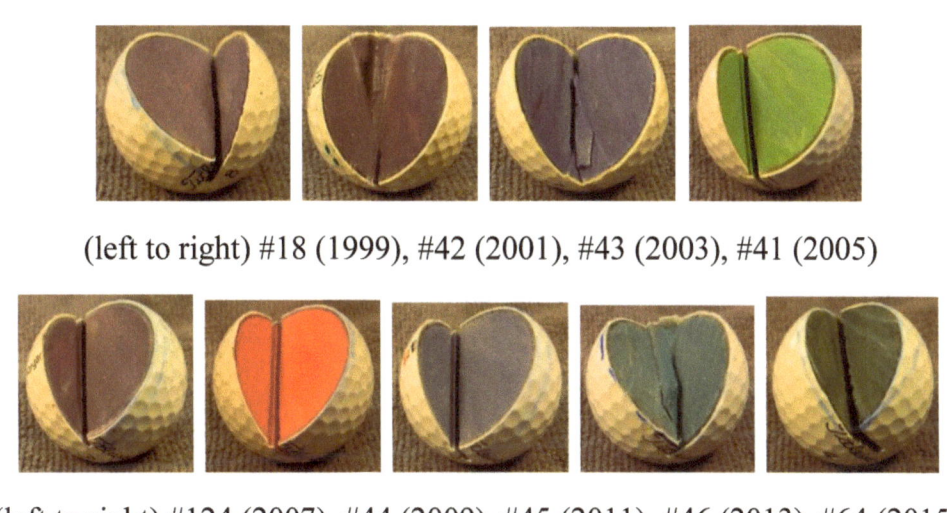

(left to right) #18 (1999), #42 (2001), #43 (2003), #41 (2005)

(left to right) #124 (2007), #44 (2009), #45 (2011), #46 (2013), #64 (2015)

Figure 11.3 Titleist Pro V1 golf balls cut open to show the core

Different color usually means some kind of change in chemical composition. The wide variety in the colors for the Pro V1 cores over the period from 1999 to 2015 very likely means that the composition of the core changed over that period of time. One possibility is that the polybutadiene (PBD) starting material used to prepare the golf ball cores was different. Acushnet Company purchased the polybutadiene (PBD) from different chemical suppliers, so this is a likely possibility. The suppliers made PBD by polymerizing butadiene using different metal catalysts such as neodymium (Nd), nickel (Ni), or Cobalt (Co). Transition metal catalysts such as Nd, Ni, and Co are known to have a variety of colors depending on a number of factors such as the oxidation state of the metal and the kind of ligands that surrounded the metal. After purchasing the PBD from their supplier, Titleist then subjected the PBD to different reagents and different chemical conditions to form the golf ball cores shown in Figure 11.3. Obviously there was a change.

The U.S. patent literature for the Titleist Pro V1 golf ball technology is reported on the Titleist website.[8] In 2002, Wu et al. obtained a patent[9] for an improved golf ball core. This patent disclosed an improved low compression (soft) golf ball with high resiliency (CoR) that was made by converting the starting polybutadiene, which had high percent cis isomer content and low percent trans isomer content, to a product polybutadiene that had high percent trans isomer content. This was done by using a cis-trans organosulfur isomerization catalyst. The product polybutadiene was then crosslinked and molded into a spherical core, which had higher hardness and higher percent trans-polybutadiene content at the surface of the core compared to the center of the core. This was called a positive hardness gradient (hardness measured at the surface minus the hardness at the center).

In 2014, Brian Comeau et al. obtained a patent[10] for a golf ball whose core had a shallow positive hardness gradient. This meant that the hardness at the surface of the core was only slightly higher than the hardness at the center of the core. The polybutadiene that was used to make the core of this golf ball was preferably made using a neodymium or cobalt catalyst. In addition, the process of forming the core also changed. Not only were the types and amounts of cis-trans isomerization catalyst, free radical initiator, antioxidant, and crosslinking agent that was present during the cure cycle changed, but also the time and temperature of the cure cycle. Lower temperatures and shorter cure times gave lower positive hardness gradients. The ratio of antioxidant to free radical initiator was one additional factor used to control the surface hardness of the core. This golf ball, whose core had a shallow hardness gradient, was an improvement over previous Pro V1 golf balls, because the core was even softer than previous versions and yet had high resiliency.

Synopsis Chapter Eleven

- The Titleist Pro V1 golf ball is a three piece ball with a single core and two covers.
- Every two years Acushnet introduced an improved version of the Titleist Pro V1 golf ball.
- The dimple pattern, the composition of the core and the cover may have changed every two years but the spin rating (M-H) has stayed the same.
- The M-H spin rating is best suited for the skilled golfer who is able to control unintentional side spin.

- The high percent trans-polybutadiene core of the Titleist Pro V1 golf ball has a shallow positive hardness gradient.
- The Titleist Pro V1 golf ball feels soft and has high resiliency.
- The seam label on the Titleist Pro V1 golf ball, as well as all other Titleist golf balls, can be used to date when the ball was introduced.

CHAPTER TWELVE
TITLEIST PRO V1X GOLF BALLS

The Pro V1x golf ball was introduced in 2003. This ball was a four-piece ball with an inner core, an outer core, an inner cover, and an outer cover.[1] The Pro V1x golf ball was fundamentally different from the Pro V1 golf ball, because the Pro V1x had two separate cores and two covers and the Pro V1 golf ball had only one core. The inner core and outer core of the Pro V1x were made by crosslinking polybutadiene (PBD) with a crosslinking agent and a free radical initiator in the presence of a filler material. The use of different amounts of filler, or different kinds of fillers (ZnO, CaO, or tungsten for example) in the inner and outer cores, resulted in separate cores that had different densities. A golf ball that had a dense (high specific gravity) inner core and low specific gravity outer core would have a low moment of inertia (MOI) and high spin. Likewise, a golf ball with a low specific gravity inner core and a high specific gravity outer core would have a high moment of inertia and low spin.

The Pro V1x golf ball had a hard ionomer inner cover and a thin soft polyurethane outer cover like the Pro V1 golf ball. The hard ionomer inner cover (sometimes called an intermediate layer) resulted in a golf ball that had low spin. The thin soft polyurethane outer cover produced a golf ball that felt soft. Figure 12.1 shows a cross section of a 4P-2c (4-piece golf ball with two covers) golf ball (10) design which shows the inner core (16), the outer core (18), the inner cover (22) and the outer cover (20).

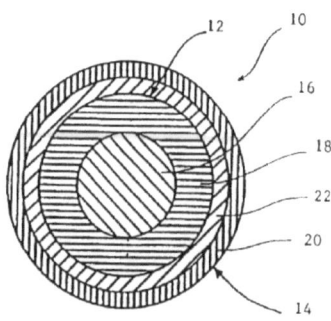

Figure 12.1 Cross section of 4P-2c golf ball[1]

notebook number	pole label	seam label	date	chpt.	dimple pattern	BALL	COVER	SPIN	diameter in.	weight oz.	seam
50	Titleist 1	< ° Pro V1x 332 ° >	2003	6	332 IE	4P	2c	M-H	1.69	1.62	
20	Titleist 4	< Pro V1x-332 >	2005	6	332 IE	4P	2c	M-H	1.69	1.62	
55	Titleist 1	<— Pro V1x —>	2007	6	332 IE	4P	2c	M-H	1.67	1.63	SW
137	Titleist 4	< ° — Pro V1x — ° >	2009	6	332 IE	4P	2c	M-H	1.68	1.62	SW
147	Titleist 1	← Pro V1x →	2011	7	328 T	4P	2c	M-H	1.69		SL
56	Titleist 4	← Pro V1x → (arrows in gray)	2013	7	328 T	4P	1c	M-H	1.68	1.61	SL
57	Titleist 3	<— Pro V1x —> (arrows in gray)	2015	7	328 T	4P	1c	M-H	1.69	1.61	SL
227	Titleist 3	<< Pro V1x >>	2017	7	328 T	4P	1c	M-H			SL

Figure 12.2 Pro V1x golf balls 2003-2017

Figure 12.2 shows the changes that have taken place for the Titleist Pro V1 golf ball over the period 2003 to 2017. Figure 12.2 contains the same information that appeared in Figure 11.2 in the previous chapter.

The different labeling on the seam of the Pro V1x golf ball every two years follows the same pattern as the labeling on the Pro V1 golf ball. In 2011, the dimple pattern for the Pro V1x golf ball changed from the 332 IE dimple pattern to the 328 T dimple pattern. The 332 IE dimple pattern had high percent surface coverage and was designed to provide long distance to golfers with very high swing speeds. The 2011, dimple pattern change probably occurred because the 332 IE golf ball would travel too far. Also the 328 T dimple pattern was adopted for the Pro V1x golf balls because the 328 T dimple pattern had improved spherical symmetry compared to the 332 IE dimple pattern.

The spin rating for the Pro V1x golf ball remained M-H over the period 2003-2017. This indicates that the Pro V1x golf ball was also designed for golfers who are able to control unintentional side spin in their golf game.

The Pro V1x was especially designed for the golfer who had very high swing speed (driver club head speed). By very high swing speed I mean swing speed in excess of about 120 mph, which is about the upper range of professional golfers swing speed (115-120 mph).

The Titleist website lists the U.S. patents for the Pro V1x golf ball. Reading these patents I found that in 2008 Hebert et al. obtained a patent[6] for a 4P 2c golf ball that had been optimized with respect to the size of the center and the outer core, the hardness of the center and the outer core, the size of the inner cover, and the hardness of the inner and outer cover. The new golf balls were tested and compared to the Pinnacle Gold LS (low spin, long distance ball) and the Tour Balata (high spin, short shot ball). The results showed that the new 4P 2c golf balls had about the same low spin and long distance as the Pinnacle gold LS ball when struck with a driver, and almost the same high spin and launch angle as the Tour Balata when struck with an 8 iron and a wedge.

In 2009 and 2017, Bulpett et al. obtained patents[7-8] for a 4P 2c golf ball that had a soft outer core and a hard inner core. This provided a golf ball with desirable 'feel' and spin characteristics. This was accomplished by adjusting the reagents and the reaction conditions for preparing the inner core and the outer core to prepare a hard inner core and a soft outer core, which was called a negative hardness gradient. The critical differences in the reagents and the reaction conditions were the ratio of the antioxidant (AO) and initiator (I) (AO/I = 0.50 to 0.57, the cure temperature (305-320°C), and the cure time (11 to 16 min.).

A golf ball that has an inner core and an outer core can exist in two different spin environments: a low spin environment and a high spin environment. In the low spin environment, the inner surface of the outer core layer is harder than the outer surface of the inner core. This is shown in Figure 12.3.

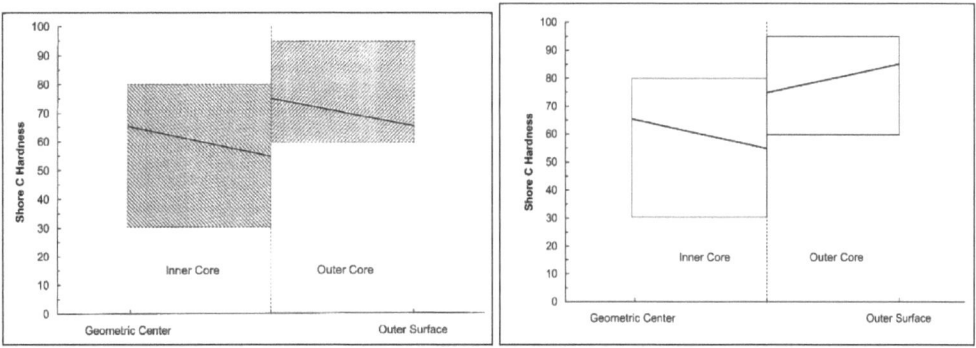

Figure 12.3 Low spin environments for a dual core golf ball[7,8]

In the high spin environment, the inner surface of the outer core layer is softer than the outer surface of the inner core. This is shown in Figure 12.4.

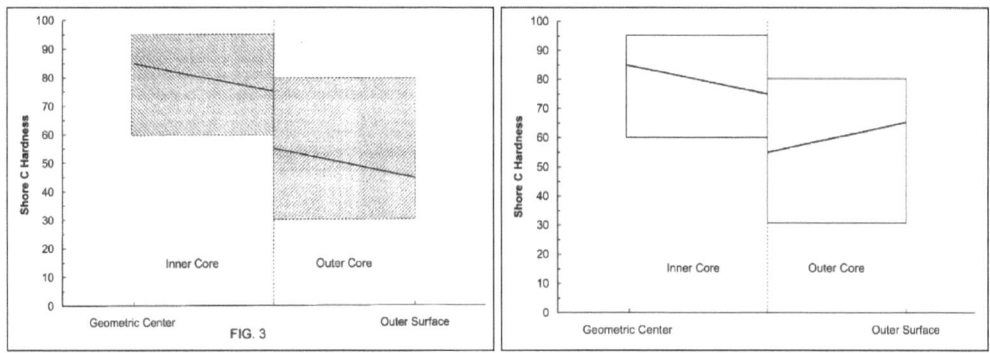

Figure 12.4 High spin environments for a dual core golf ball[7,8]

In 2015, Sullivan et al. obtained a patent[9] for a dual core golf ball that had a shallow positive hardness gradient for the inner core or center of the golf ball and a positive hardness gradient for the outer core. This was accomplished by optimizing the amount of antioxidant and the conditions for cross-linking the polybutadiene to form the inner and outer cores. The hardness of the inner core and for the outer core as a function of distance from the golf ball center is shown in Figure 12.5.

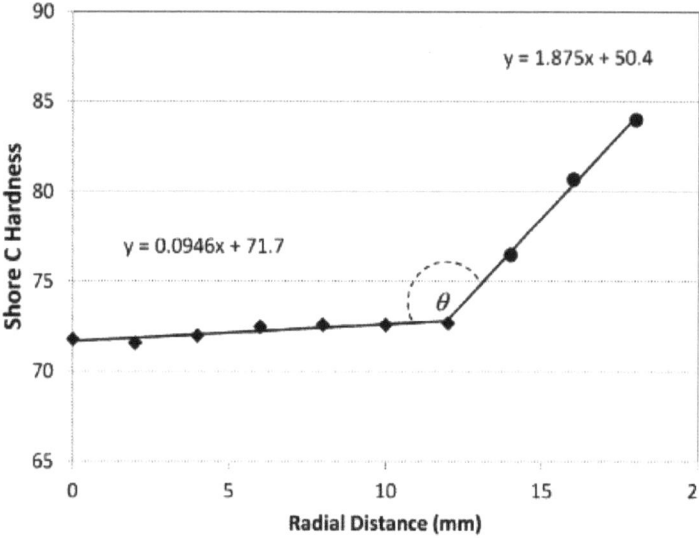

Figure 12.5 Hardness Gradient for a Dual Core Golf Ball such as Pro V1x[9]

Synopsis Chapter Twelve

- The Titleist Pro V1x golf ball is a four piece ball with two cores and two covers.
- The Titleist Pro V1x golf ball was designed for the golfer with very high swing speeds.
- A golf ball with a dual core can be made with either a high spin or a low spin embodiment simply by modifying the relative hardness of the inner and the outer cores.
- The spin rating of the Titleist Pro V1x is M-H.
- This spin rating is best suited for the skilled golfer who is able to control unintentional side spin.

Chapter Thirteen
Titleist NXT, AVX, Tour Soft Golf Balls
Titleist NXT Tour

In 2002, Ladd et al, obtained a patent[1] for a multilayer golf ball that was soft (low compression) and also had high resiliency (CoR). For this three-piece ball a new core was developed, which consisted of a center and an outer core. The center consisted of a mixture of cis-polybutadiene (PBD), a cis-trans catalyst, a free radical initiator, a cross-linking agent, and a density modifier that were mixed together and heated to mold the spherical core of the golf ball. During the molding cycle, an amount of the cis-polybutadiene was converted to trans-polybutadiene to produce a core that was softer than the core that was molded using only cispolybutadiene. Unexpectedly, the resiliency of the core remained high.[2] The outer core (also called an intermediate layer) consisted of the high percent trans-PBD core mixture described above, plus a reinforcing polymer. Suitable reinforcing polymers included trans-polyisoprene (balata), polyethylene, or a thermoplastic polyester (e.g., HYTREL). Figure 13.1 shows a cross section of the NXT Tour golf ball (three-piece, one cover).

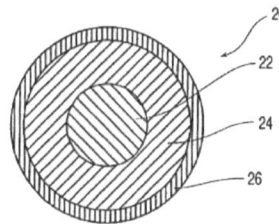

Figure 13.1 3P 1c golf ball (20), cover (26), intermediate layer (24), center (22)[1]

An automated method for making these multilayered cores for golf balls appeared in 2003.[3] Figure 13.2 shows the changes that have taken place in the Titleist NXT Tour golf ball from the period 2001 to the present.

notebook number	pole label	seam label	date	chpt.	dimple pattern	BALL	COVER	SPIN	diameter in.	weight oz.	seam
12	Titleist 1	< NXT ∘ Tour >	2001	3	392 IC2	2P	1c	M-H	1.69		
128	Titleist 1	< NXT Tour >	2003	5	392 ID	2P	1c	M-H	1.68		
142	Titleist 1	< NXT - Tour >	2005	5	392 ID	3P	1c	L-M	1.68		
158	Titleist 3	<— NXT Tour —>	2007	5	392 ID	3P	1c	L-M	1.69	1.62	SW
125	Titleist 2	< ∘ — NXT Tour — ∘ >	2009	6	332 IE	3P	1c	L-M	1.68	1.62	SW
160	Titleist 3	←NXT Tour→	2011	7	302 CO	3P	1c	L-M	1.69	1.62	SL
59	Titleist 3	← NXT Tour → (arrows in gray)	2013	7	302 CO	3P	1c	L-M	1.67	1.61	SL
159	Titleist 3	<—NXT Tour—> (arrows in gray)	2015	7	302 CO	3P	1c	L-M	1.69	1.61	SL
226	Titleist 2	<< AVX >>	2018	7	352 T	3P	1c	L-M	1.69		SL

Figure 13.2 Titleist NXT Tour and AVX golf balls

The earliest NXT Tour golf ball that I have in my collection (ball #12), which was introduced in 2001, had the 392 IC2 dimple pattern. Between 2001 and 2003 the dimple pattern changed from the 392 IC2 dimple pattern to the 392 ID pattern. The 2001 and 2003 NXT Tour golf balls both were two-piece balls with one cover that had a spin rating of M-H. They seem to be in a class all their own.

Then, from 2005 to 2015, the NXT Tour golf balls were three-piece balls with one cover that had a spin rating of L-M. In 2007, Titleist introduced the staggered wave (SW) technology (Chapter 6) for the NXT Tour golf ball models. The SW technology was developed so the asymmetry due to the parting line at the seam of the 392 ID dimple pattern could be eliminated. In 2009, the dimple pattern changed to the 332 IE dimple pattern which traveled farther than the 392 ID pattern. In 2011, the new USGA distance and symmetry rules took effect. In that year the Titleist changed the 332 IE dimple pattern to the 302 CO dimple pattern so the USGA symmetry rule would not be violated. At the same time seamless (SL) parting line technology (Chapter 7) was also introduced. In order to meet the USGA distance rule in 2011, Titleist must have changed either the CoR of the core, the dimple diameter, edge angle, or percent surface coverage, because when I measured the golf ball diameters and weights, I found little, if any, change from the USGA standard diameter and weight.

The Titleist AVX golf ball is included in Figure 13.2 with the Titleist NXT Tour golf balls. This golf ball was first introduced in 2017. It is a three-piece ball with one cover, the spin rating is L-M, and it has 352 dimples arranged in a tetrahedral dimple pattern. I believe the new AVX ball replaces the NXT Tour golf ball models. The printed information on the AVX box indicates that the dimples on the AVX golf balls have a catenary dimple design (Chapter 6).

NXT, NXT Extreme, NXT Tour S, and TOUR SOFT golf balls

The technology for the NXT, NXT Extreme, NXT Tour S, and the TOUR SOFT golf balls was different than the technology for the NXT Tour golf ball. These golf balls were all two-piece balls with a single cover. In 2003, Cavallaro et al. obtained a patent[4] for a low golf spin ball that had good distance and a soft cover for softer feel. The large solid core for this ball was made by cross-linking polybutadiene with zinc diacrylate and a free radical initiator, in the presence of CaO activation agent. The results of this study showed that the golf ball containing CaO produced a softer core with no decrease in the initial velocity compared to the golf ball containing ZnO activation agent. The golf ball cores also included fillers, which adjusted the density (specific gravity) of the core. One filler that was preferred in the Cavallaro patent was tungsten powder. Tungsten is a dense material that was added to the golf ball to increase the density of the core.

The soft cover for the NXT Tour S golf ball was a mixture of two materials each having different softness (flexural moduli). One example of a soft cover disclosed in the Cavallaro patent consisted of a blend of an ionomer and a metallocene catalyzed polymer, for example polyethylene. Another example of a soft cover consisted of a blend of two different ionomers and FUSABOND®, a polymer made by du Pont Company.

Figure 13.3 shows a cross section of the NXT Tour S golf ball (10), where 11 is the large PBD core and 12 is the soft cover.

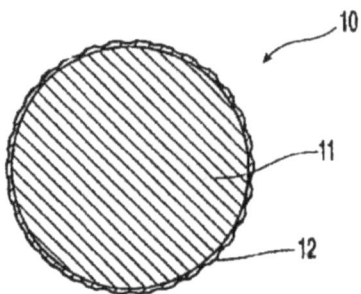

Figure 13.3 Cross section of NXT Tour S golf balls (2p 1c)[4]

Figure 13.4 shows the changes that have taken place for the Titleist NXT, the NXT Distance, the NXT Extreme, and the NXT Tour S, over the period 2001 to the present. My golf ball collection is missing many of the different models for many different years during that time period.

The 2001 NXT Distance model was a two-piece ball with a single cover and a spin rating of L-M. This ball had the 392 ID dimple pattern, which continued to be used on the NXT and the NXT Extreme models over the period from 2005 to 2007. The NXT Extreme golf ball incorporated the staggered wave parting technology in 2007 as did the NXT golf ball with the 332 IE dimple pattern produced in 2009.

The earliest NXT Tour S golf ball that I have in my collection is from the year 2011. I think this was the year of its introduction. The NXT Tour S golf balls were all two-piece golf balls with one cover that had the symmetric 302 CO dimple pattern. The spin rating was L-M. In 2011, the NXT Tour S golf ball used the seamless parting line technology (SL) to meet the symmetry standard as well as modification of the CoR of the core, the dimple diameter, edge angle, or percent surface coverage to meet the USGA distance standard.

In 2017, Titleist introduced the new TOUR SOFT golf ball to replace the NXT Tour S. This golf ball had 342 dimples that were arranged in a cuboctahedral dimple pattern. This was a two-piece ball with one cover, and had an L-M spin rating.

GOLF BALL COVER STORY

notebook number	pole label	seam label	date	chpt.	dimple pattern	BALL	COVER	SPIN	diameter in.	weight oz.	seam
126	Titleist 4	< NXT ○ Distance >	2001	5	392 ID	2P	1c	L-M	1.68	1.61	
14	Titleist 2	< NXT >	2003	5	392 ID	2P	1c	L-M	1.68	1.61	
155	Titleist 4	<— NXT —>	2005	5	392 ID	2P	1c	L-M	1.69	1.61	
157	Titleist 2	<— NXT Extreme —>	2007	5	392 ID	2P	1c	L-M	1.69	1.61	SW
156	Titleist 2	< ○ — NXT — ○ >	2009	6	332 IE	2P	1c	L-L	1.69	1.61	SW
150	Titleist 2	← NXT Tour S →	2011	7	302 CO	2P	1c	L-M	1.69	1.61	SL
60	Titleist 2	← NXT Tour S → (arrows in gray)	2013	7	302 CO	2P	1c	L-M	1.67	1.61	SL
61	Titleist 4	← NXT Tour S → (arrows in gray)	2013	7	302 CO	2P	1c	L-M	1.67	1.61	SL
248	Titleist 1	<< TOUR SOFT >>	2018	7	342 CO	2P	1c	L-M			SL

Figure 13.4 Titleist NXT, NXT Extreme, NXT Tour S, and TOUR SOFT golf balls

Synopsis Chapter Thirteen

- The Titleist NXT Tour golf ball is a three piece ball with one cover.
- The spin rating for the Titleist NXT Tour ball was L-M.
- This ball spins less rapidly than the Pro V1 or the Pro V1x and may be suitable for the golfer who can sometimes control unintentional side spin.
- The Titleist AVX golf ball was introduced in 2017 to replace the Titleist NXT Tour model.
- The Titleist NXT Tour S golf ball is a two piece ball with one core and one cover.
- The Titleist NXT Tour S has a spin rating of L-M.
- The Titleist Tour Soft was introduced in 2018 to replace the Titleist NXT Tour S.

Chapter Fourteen
Titleist Tour, Velocity Golf Balls

The Titleist Tour model was first introduced in the 1980s with the Titleist *384 Tour 100* model which traveled farther than other golf balls at that time. The Titleist Tour was introduced in 1991, the Tour Prestige (a British ball) in 1990, the Tour Balata, in 1994, and the Professional model in 1995. These golf balls were all wound with a liquid center and a soft balata cover except for the Professional, which used a polyurethane cover.

Figure 14.1 shows the changes that have taken place for the Titleist Tour golf ball models over the period 1984 to 1995.

Professional golfers preferred to use golf balls that felt soft and had high spin so they could stop the ball quickly on the green when struck with a high lofted club. In the 1990s, the Titleist Tour Balata and the Professional golf balls met these needs. These wound balls with a liquid center and balata (B) or urethane (U) covers, felt soft, traveled almost as far as a two-piece ball, and had high spin. The Tour Balata ball, which was introduced in 1994, was desired for its soft feel and high spin. The Tour Balata was a wound ball with a liquid center and 392 dimples arranged in the 392 IC dimple pattern. The Titleist Professional golf ball, introduced in 1995, was different from the Tour Balata because it had a polyurethane cover. This cover was more durable than the balata cover, but just as soft. Tiger Woods won many of his early Tournament victories using the Titleist Professional golf ball.

One ball, #17 the Tour Prestige 100, had a diameter of only 1.64 inches. This indicates it was a smaller British ball. Ball #3, the *384 TOUR 100*, was a wound ball with a liquid center and a balata cover. It was introduced in 1984 and had 384 dimples arranged in the original icosahedron dimple pattern. This ball was designed to give the professional golfer longer distance compared to the golf balls that were available at the time. The longer distance was the result of using a 1 1/8 inch liquid core and a harder balata cover (Chapter 2).

Figure 14.2 shows the changes that have taken place for the Titleist Tour Distance and Titleist Velocity golf balls over the period 1998 to the present.

notebook number	pole label	seam label	date	chpt.	dimple pattern	BALL	CENTER	COVER	diameter in.	notes
3	Titleist 7	* 384 TOUR 100 *	1984	2	384 IB	W	LC	B	1.67	
15	Titleist 3	* Tour 100 *	1991	3	392 ICI	W	LC	B	1.67	
131	Titleist 6	* TOUR 90 *	1991	3	392 ICI	W	LC	B	1.66	
17	Titleist 1	Tour Prestige 100	1990	3	392 ICI	W	LC		1.64	small
70	Titleist 3	Tour Balata Δ 90	1994	3	392 ICI	W	LC	B	1.66	
135	Titleist 2	Tour Balata Δ 100	1994	3	392 ICI	W	LC	B	1.67	
134	Titleist 2	Professional 90	1995	3	392 ICI	W	LC	U	1.66	
5	Titleist 1	Professional Δ 90	1995	3	392 ICI	W	LC	U	1.65	
86	Titleist 1	Professional 100	1995	3	392 ICI	W	LC	U	1.67	
164	Titleist 1	Professional Δ 100	1995	3	392 ICI	W	LC	U	1.65	

Figure 14.1 Titleist Tour models and Titleist Professional golf balls

Golf Ball Cover Story

notebook number	pole label	seam label	date	chpt.	dimple pattern	BALL	CENTER	COVER	SPIN	diameter in.	weight oz.	seam notes	
16	Titleist 2	Tour Distance 100	1998	3	392 IC2	W	LC			1.69			
40	Titleist 1	Tour Distance-90	1998	3	392 IC2	W	LC			1.67			
21	Titleist 1	<Tour Distance SF >	2001	3	392 IC2	2P				1.67			
63	Titleist 3	<Tour Prestige >	1999	5	392 ID	2P	SC	1c	L-M	1.69			
127	Titleist 2	<— Tour Distance —>	2007	5	392 ID	2P	SC	1c	M-H	1.69	1.62	SW	
163	Titleist 4	<°— Tour Distance —° >	2009	6	332 IE	2P	SC	1c	L-M	1.69	1.61	SW	
170	Titleist 3	←Velocity →	2011	6	332 IE	2P	SC	1c	L-L	1.69	1.60	SW	light
22	Titleist 33	←Velocity → (arrows in gray)	2013	7	328 T	2P	SC	1c	L-L	1.69	1.60	SL	light
98	Titleist 99	<—Velocity —> (arrows in gray)	2015	7	328 T	2P	SC	1c	L-L	1.68	1.61	SL	
	Titleist	<<Velocity >>	2017	7	328 T	2P	SC	1c	L-L			SL	

Figure 14.2 Tour Distance and Velocity Golf Balls

The Tour Prestige makes its appearance again in 1999. In contrast to the Tour Prestige shown in Figure 14.1, this ball was a two-piece ball with a single cover and it had 392 dimples arranged in the 392 ID dimple pattern. This Tour Prestige had the normal diameter of 1.69 inches and an L-M spin rating.

The Titleist Tour Distance was introduced around 1998. It was a wound ball with a liquid center and it had 392 dimple arranged in an icosahedron dimple pattern (392 IC). In 2001, the Tour Distance balls started using two-piece technology with a solid core and a single cover. The 2001 Tour Distance SF was a softer version of the 1998 Tour Distance ball. It is apparent that Figure 14.2 is missing several different golf ball models over the time period 1998-2007.

In 2007, the Tour Distance golf ball had the 392 ID dimple pattern, the spin rating was M-H, and the ball used the staggered wave technology (Chapter 6) to improve flight symmetry. These golf balls continued to be produced through 2009 with two-piece construction, 332 IE dimple pattern, a single cover, staggered wave (SW) technology, and L-M spin rating.

In 2011, The Titleist Velocity golf ball replaced the Tour Distance model. The Titleist Velocity model was a two-piece ball with a single cover. It had an L-L spin rating and the 332 IE dimple pattern, but its claim to fame was that it had the highest velocity core of any Titleist golf ball. In order to meet the USGA distance standard, Titleist had to reduce the weight of the Velocity golf ball in 2011 and 2013. In addition, in order to meet the symmetry standard, the 2011 Titleist Velocity golf ball not only used the staggered wave technology but also had modified dimples on the ball (Chapter 7) since the 332 IE dimple pattern was not spherically symmetrical. In 2013 the Velocity model began using the symmetrical 328 T dimple pattern with seamless (SL) parting line design.

The Titleist Velocity golf ball has low spin with the driver and the lofted iron (L-L spin rating). For that reason it is often preferred by a golfer who has difficulty controlling unintentional side spin.

Synopsis Chapter Fourteen

- The Titleist Tour family of golf balls can be traced all the way back to the 1990's with the introduction of the Tour Balata, Professional, and the Tour Distance.
- The Titleist Velocity golf ball was introduced in 2011 and is a two piece ball with a single cover.
- The spin rating for the Titleist Velocity is L-L which may be attractive for the golfer who is less able to control unintentional side spin.
- Because of its high velocity core, the Titleist Velocity golf ball was made lighter in weight to pass the USGA distance rule.

CHAPTER FIFTEEN
TITLEIST DT GOLF BALLS

On the Titleist DT golf ball the 'DT' stood for 'Distance Titleist'. In the 1970's, the 'DT' label on the DT Titleist stood for 'Durable Titleist' (Chapter 2). Figure 15.1 contains the Titleist DT golf balls that were made from about 1991 to about 2000. The Titleist DT golf balls were very popular with the recreational golfer because of the long distance and durable cover.

Figure 15.1 shows the changes that have taken place for the Titleist DT golf ball over the period 1991 to 2000.

notebook number	pole label	seam label	date	chpt.	dimple pattern	BALL	COVER	diameter in.
8	Titleist 2	* DT 100 *	1991	3	392 IC1	W	S	1.69
77	Titleist 3	* DT 90 *	1991	3	392 IC2	W	S	1.67
90	Titleist 2	DT Δ 90	1991	3	392 IC2	W	S	1.68
94	Titleist 4	* DT 80 *	1991	3	392 IC2	W	S	1.68
95	Titleist 2	DT Δ Wound 80	1996	3	392 IC2	W	S	1.68
9	Titleist 3	Δ DT Δ Wound 90	1996	3	392 IC2	W	S	1.67
52	Titleist 4	Δ DT Δ Wound 100	1996	3	392 IC2	W	S	1.68
10	Titleist 1	DT Δ 2-Piece	1996	3	392 IC2	2P	S	1.69
49	Titleist 2	Δ DT Δ 2-Piece	1996	3	392 IC2	2P	S	1.69
19	Titleist 3	< DT Distance >	2000	3	392 IC2	2P	1c	1.69
168	Titleist 4	DT ○ Distance	2000	5	392 ID	2P	1c	1.69

Figure 15.1 Early Titleist DT golf ball models from about 1991 to 2000

The Titleist DT golf balls (1991-1996) were wound balls (W) with a solid rubber center, and they had 392 dimples arranged in an icosahedron dimple pattern (392 IC). They had a durable Surlyn cover (S). Ball #8 is labeled with the dimple pattern 392 IC1, because the pole label was located exactly at the pole and the seam label exactly at the seam of the icosahedron dimple patterns. All the other balls (392 IC2) have the pole label and seam label randomly placed on the icosahedron dimple pattern. The 80 compression Titleist DT balls were

notebook number	pole label	seam label	date	chpt.	dimple pattern	BALL	COVER	SPIN	diameter in.	weight oz.	seam	swing speed	notes
114	Titleist 3	DT SofLo	2003	5	392 ID	2P	1c	L-M	1.67				
11	Titleist 1	< DT SofLo >	2005	5	392 ID	2P	1c	L-M	1.68				
38	Titleist 4	<— DT Roll —>	2007	5	392 ID	2P	1c	L-M	1.69	1.62	SW		
79	Titleist 2	<— DT Carry —>	2007	6	252 I	2P	1c	L-M	1.68	1.59	SW		light
88	Titleist 2	<— DT SoLo —>	2007	5	392 ID	2P	1c	L-M	1.68	1.62	SW		
91	Titleist 1	<— DT SoLo —>	2011	5	392 ID	2P	1c	L-M	1.68	1.59	SW	slow	light
165	Titleist 2	<— DT Solo —>	2011	5	392 ID	2P	1c	L-M	1.69	1.58	SW	slow	light
53	Titleist 2	<— DT Solo —> (arrows in gray)	2013	7	376 T	2P	1c	L-M	1.68	1.59	SL	slow	light
62	Titleist 1	<—DT Trusoft —> (arrows in gray)	2015	7	376 T	2P	1c	L-M	1.68	1.60	SL	slow	light
229	Titleist 3	<— DT Trusoft —> (arrows in gray)	2015	7	376 T	2P	1c	L-M			SL	slow	light

Figure 15.2 Titleist DT Models after 2000

designed for the low swing speed golfer, the 90 compression for the average swing speed golfer, and the 100 compression for the high swing speed golfer. There are three different seam labels on the Titleist DT golf balls that may indicate changes were made every couple of years. The name on the seam appears to change with time as follows: *DT 90* (earliest), DT Δ 90 (later), Δ DT Δ 90 (latest). In 1996, Titleist introduced the DT 2-Piece golf balls, which were two-piece golf balls with a Surlyn cover. The Titleist DT Distance golf ball, which had the same basic construction as the Titleist DT 2-piece, was introduced in 2000. This ball had the 392 ID dimple pattern, which traveled farther than the 392 IC dimple pattern.

Figure 15.2 shows the changes that have been made to the Titleist DT SoLo over the period 2003 to the present. Also included in Figure 15.2 are the Titleist DT Roll and the Titleist DT Carry golf balls.

In 2003, Titleist introduced the DT SoLo ball. This ball was a two-piece ball with a single cover, the 392 ID dimple pattern, and an L-M spin rating. It continued to be produced from 2003 until 2013. In 2015 the DT SoLo model was replaced by the DT Trusoft model. Often the DT SoLo and the DT Trusoft weighed less than the maximum weight standard for golf balls (1.62 oz). This was because the DT SoLo was a ball for a player with a low swing speed (Chapter 9).

The DT Carry (252 I dimple pattern), which was introduced in 2007, was a two-piece ball that had a single cover and an L-M spin rating. This ball was designed for a player with a high swing speed. The dimples on the DT Carry had large diameters and high percent surface coverage, and as a result, the total dimple volume was high. This resulted in a low coefficient of lift, low spin, and a low trajectory resulting in long distance.

The DT Roll golf ball was a two-piece ball with 392 dimples and a single cover.

Synopsis Chapter Fifteen

- The Titleist DT family of golf balls can be traced all the way back to the 1990's with the Titleist DT Wound, the Titleist DT 2-piece, and the Titleist DT Distance models.
- The Titleist DT Solo golf ball was made for the player with a low swing speed.
- The Titleist DT Solo and the Titleist DT Trusoft golf ball, which replaced the Titleist DT Solo, were made lighter in weight to benefit the golfer with a low swing speed.

Chapter Sixteen
Pinnacle Golf Balls

Pinnacle golf balls have been around for about as long as Titleist golf balls. Acushnet Company began producing the Acushnet 'Pinnacle' golf ball in the early 1940's as a low cost golf ball for the average golfer. The 'Pinnacle' golf ball, along with the model names 'Finalist', 'Titleist', 'Green Ray', and 'Bradford', had the name 'Acushnet', plus two circles with center dots on one pole, and the model name plus two circles with center dots on the other pole. This was discussed and photos of the Acushnet Titleist and the Acushnet Finalist were included in Chapter 1.

One way to help golf ball collectors assign a date to the Pinnacle golf balls is to realize that starting in about 1973, Pinnacle started to regularly change the Pinnacle pole logo. First, the old Pinnacle logo (OPL, 1973-1989)[1] was used. The next pole label was called the flag pin logo (FP, 1989-2002)[2], followed by the airfoil logo (AL, 2002-2007)[3], the airfoil jet logo (AJ, 2007-2013)[4], and finally the jet trail logo (JT, 2013-present).

Photographs of the Pinnacle Golf Ball Logos

Figure 16.1 left to right (OPL, FP, AL, AJ, JT logos)

Figure 16.2 shows the changes that have taken place for the Pinnacle golf balls that have the Old Pinnacle Logo. These balls were produced from about 1973-1989.

OLD PINNACLE LOGO

notebook number	pole label	seam label	date	chpt.	dimple pattern	BALL	COVER	SPIN	diameter in.
13	PINNACLE 5	Pinnacle	1983	2	324 IA	**2P**	**B**		1.68
31	384 PINNACLE 2	90 Compression	1987	2	384 IB	2P	B		1.69
100	384 Pinnacle 2	90 COMPRESSION	1987	2	384 IB	2P	B		1.68
99	PINNACLE 1	Pinnacle 90	1987	3	332 IA	2P			1.68
32	4 PINNACLE Gold		1989	3	392 IC2	2P			1.69
249	Pinnacle 2		1989	3	392 IC2	2P			

Figure 16.2 Pinnacle golf balls with the Old Pinnacle Logo (OPL)

The Pinnacle golf ball is known for long distance, low spin, a durable cover, and low price. This golf ball has been very popular with the recreational golfer. One very well known model is the Pinnacle Gold. This golf ball has been produced since 1989. All Pinnacle golf balls are two-piece golf balls that have low spin with the driver and low spin with a lofted iron (L-L). Golfers who have trouble controlling unintentional side spin (slice and hook), prefer to play with Pinnacle golf balls. They also like the durable cover, which suffers less damage when struck by a cart path or the limb of a tree. The early Pinnacle golf balls had a hard, durable Surlyn cover, but more recent models have a softer version.

FLAGPIN LOGO

notebook number	pole label	seam label	date	chpt.	dimple pattern	BALL	COVER	diameter in.	weight oz.	notes
33	PINNACLE 4	332	1995	2	332 IA	2P		1.69		
116	Pinnacle 4	392 LS	1999	2	392 IB	2P	S	1.68	1.60	
149	Pinnacle 2	PERFORMANCE	1997	5	392 ID	2P		1.69	1.63	heavy
112	SUPER Pinnacle Plus 1		1996		372 I	2P		1.72	1.62	large
72	Pinnacle 4	Gold	1998	3	392 IC2	2P		1.68		
71	Pinnacle 4	Extreme	1999	3	392 IC2	2P		1.68		
73	Pinnacle 2	> Gold LS	1999	5	392 ID	2P		1.68		
74	Pinnacle 2	Gold LS	1999	5	392 ID	2P		1.67		
113	Pinnacle Titanium 1	> Extreme	1999	4	440 CO	2P		1.68	1.62	
117	Pinnacle 2	Gold Distance	1999	5	392 ID	2P		1.68	1.61	
93	Pinnacle 2	> Power 392	2000	3	392 IC2	2P		1.68	1.60	
103	Pinnacle 4	Gold Spin	2002	5	392 ID	2P	1c	1.68	1.61	
101	Pinnacle 1	Gold-Ex	2002	5	392 ID	2P		1.68	1.61	
228	Pinnacle Titanium 4	Precision Spin	2001	4	440 CO					

Figure 16.3 Pinnacle golf balls with the Flag Pin Logo (FPL)

AIRFOIL LOGO

notebook number	pole label	seam label	date	chpt.	dimple pattern	BALL	COVER	SPIN	diameter in.	weight oz.	Dimple Profile
106	PINNACLE 2		2002	3	392 IC2	2P			1.68	1.61	
182	PINNACLE 2	ɣ GOLD LADY	2001	5	392 ID	2P	1c	L-L	1.69	1.56	
107	PINNACLE 4	Gold ○ Distance	2002	5	392 ID	2P	1c	L-L	1.69	1.61	
108	PINNACLE 2	Gold Distance	2002	5	392 ID	2P		L-L	1.69		
109	Pinnacle Gold 4	<< >	2002	5	392 ID	2P	1c	L-L	1.68	1.61	
110	Pinnacle Gold 1	<< >	2002	5	392 ID	2P	1c	L-L	1.68	1.61	
171	PINNACLE 3	POWER CORE	2002	3	392 IC2	2P	1c	L-L	1.68	1.62	
178	PINNACLE 3	TITANIUM DISTANCE	2002	3	392 ID	2P	1c	L-L	1.69	1.60	
175	PINNACLE POWER CORE 3	STRAIGHT DISTANCE	2002	4	440 CO	2P			1.68	1.62	
174	PINNACLE 1	ɣ	2003	3	392 IC2	2P			1.68	1.62	
133	PINNACLE Exception 4	<< >	2005	5	392 ID	2P	1c	L-M	1.69	1.61	
181	PINNACLE 1	HOT ○ SHOT	2006	3	392 IC2	2P	1c	L-L	1.69	1.62	
111	PINNACLE Long Drive 3	<< >	2006	7	330 IE1*	2P	1c	L-L	1.69	1.61	M
177	PINNACLE CLR 3	<< >	2006	5	392 ID	2P	1c	L-L	1.69	1.61	

Figure 16.4 Pinnacle golf balls with the Airfoil Logo (AL)

AIRFOIL JET LOGO

notebook number	pole label	seam label	date	chpt.	dimple pattern	BALL	COVER	SPIN	diameter in.	weight oz.	Dimple Profile
104	PINNACLE Ribbon 4	Susan Kommen for the cure	2008	5	392 ID	2P	1c	L-L	1.69	1.61	
105	PINNACLE GOLD 3	<<FX SOFT >	2008	5	392 ID	2P	1c	L-L	1.69	1.61	
123	PINNACLE GOLD 1	<< FX LONG >	2008	7	330 IE1*	2P	1c	L-L	1.67	1.62	M
183	PINNACLE Ribbon 4	Susan Kommen for the cure	2010	5	392 ID	2P	1c	L-L	1.69	1.59	
186	PINNACLE GOLD 2	<<PRECISION >	2010	5	392 ID	2P	1c	L-L	1.69		
187	PINNACLE GOLD 3	<< PRECISION >	2010	5	392 ID	2P	1c	L-L	1.69	1.61	
120	PINNACLE Platinum 3	<<Feel>	2008	6	332 IE	2P	1c	L-L	1.68	1.62	
176	PINNACLE PLATINUM 2	<< Distance >	2008	6	332 IE	2P	1c	L-L	1.69	1.62	
148	Pinnacle Gold 3	<< Distance >	2010	6	332 IE	2P	1c	L-L	1.69	1.60	
121	PINNACLE 3	<<Dimension>	2010	6	332 IE	2P	1c	L-M	1.69	1.61	
119	PINNACLE 1	Exception	2012	6	332 IE	2P	1c	L-M	1.69	1.61	M
179	PINNACLE 3	<< Gold >	2012	6	332 IE	2P	1c	L-L	1.69	1.60	M
184	PINNACLE GOLD RIBBON 2	γ	2012	6	332 IE	2P	1c	L-L	1.69	1.59	M
185	PINNACLE 4	<<BLING>>	2014	6	332 IE	2P	1c	L-L	1.69	1.62	M
118	Pinnacle 4	<<Gold>>	**2015**	6	332 IE	2P	1c	L-L	1.69	1.62	M

Figure 16.5 Pinnacle golf balls with the Airfoil Jet Logo (AJ)

Figure 16.3 shows the changes that have taken place for the Pinnacle golf balls that have the flag pin logo. These golf balls were produced from about 1989 to about 2002.

The dimple pattern for the Pinnacle golf balls varied over the years. The first Pinnacle golf balls had the ATTI dimple pattern. This dimple pattern changed to the 332 IA, 392 IB, 392 IC, 392 ID, and 440 CO as the technology changed. For a time, the Pinnacle Gold was the standard golf ball for USGA testing.

Figure 16.4 shows the changes that have taken place for the Pinnacle golf balls that have the airfoil logo. These golf balls were produced from about 1996 to about 2006.

Pinnacle marketed and sold golf balls made especially for the low swing speed market. The Pinnacle γ and the Pinnacle γ GOLD LADY were introduced in the late 1990's and early 2000's, and they were followed by the PINNACLE *Ribbon* Susan G. Komen for the cure in the middle of the 2000's. This ball, # 183, weighed less than the standard 1.62 oz. weight.

Figure 16.5 shows the changes that have taken place for the Pinnacle golf balls that have the airfoil jet logo. These golf balls were produced from about 2007 to about 2016.

The PINNACLE GOLD RIBBON γ was a ball for a slow swing speed player that also weighed less than the standard 1.62 oz. weight. The PINNACLE BLING golf ball was also a ball for a slow swing speed player. Ball #179, the PINNACLE GOLD golf ball, also weight less than the standard 1.62 oz. weight, but this was for a different reason—the ball would travel too far and otherwise would violate the USGA distance rule.

Figure 16.6 shows the changes that have taken place for the Pinnacle golf balls with the jet trail logo. These golf balls were produced from about 2106 to the present.

JET TRAIL LOGO											
notebook number	pole label	seam label	date	chpt.	dimple pattern	BALL	COVER	SPIN	diameter in.	weight oz.	Dimple Profile
78	P PINNACLE 4	— Rush —	2016	6	332 IE	2P	1c	L-L	1.68	1.61	M
188	P PINNACLE 2	— SOFT —	2016	6	332 IE	2P	1c	L-L	1.69	1.62	M

Figure 16.6 Pinnacle golf Balls with the Jet Trail Logo (JT)

The two Pinnacle golf balls still being sold today are the PINNACLE RUSH and the PINNACLE SOFT. These golf balls have the same basic construction as the PINNACLE GOLD golf ball but some dimple profiles were modified (M) to make the ball spherically symmetrical (Chapter 7). The golf balls were also modified by either changing the percent surface coverage or by lowering the CoR (Chapter 8), so they would still meet the USGA distance standard. The PINNACLE SOFT probably also has a softer ionomer cover than the PINNACLE RUSH.

Synopsis Chapter Sixteen

- Pinnacle golf balls go all the way back to the 1940's.
- Pinnacle golf balls are the less expensive models made by Acushnet.
- They are all two piece balls with a solid core and a single cover.
- The Pinnacle Gold golf ball is a well know golf ball that traveled far, had L-L spin rating and had a durable Surlyn cover.
- The Pinnacle Soft and the Pinnacle Rush replaced the Pinnacle Gold golf ball.

Chapter Seventeen
Vintage Golf Balls

Acushnet Company began producing golf balls starting in about 1935. In this chapter I am going to summarize the information I have obtained about the vintage golf ball models. These are identified by the name that appears on the seam of the golf ball. I have obtained this information by visually inspecting the golf ball, reading numerous books[1-3], searching for information on the internet, finding data in older USGA conforming golf ball lists[4], and from various other sources. The information in this chapter is probably more valuable to the avid golf ball collector than to the player because many of these golf balls are collector's items and a few of them can still be found on golf courses hidden in ponds or in the rough. Many of them, however, are available to purchase on various websites on the internet such as E-Bay. So, an accurate date of production for these golf balls may help the golf ball collector determine an appropriate price for the item that they are interested in purchasing.

Figure 17.1 shows the changes that have taken place for the Vintage Titleist golf balls that have the ATTI dimple pattern (336A).

These golf balls are all wound (W) golf balls with a liquid/solid rubber center and a balata (B) cover. The page in my golf ball notebook where these golf balls are recorded is also listed in the figure, as well as the name on the pole and the seam of the ball. Photos and additional discussion about these golf balls appear in Chapter 1. These are among the oldest golf balls in my collection.

Figure 17.2 shows the changes that have taken place for the original icosahedron golf ball with 324 dimples (324 IA) and the original icosahedron golf ball with 384 dimples (384 IB).

These golf balls were produced over the period 1973 to about 1999.

notebook number	pole label	seam label	date	chpt.	dimple pattern	BALL	COVER
69	Titleist Professional 3	Acushnet, Geer Patent Cover	1935	1	336 A	W	B
47	Acushnet Finalist	Cadwell Geer D7	1939	1	336 A	W	B
97	Acushnet Titleist	Cadwell Geer Cover, For Experts Only	1939	1	336 A	W	B
39	Titleist Acushnet 4	Cadwell Geer Cover	1942	1	336 A	W	B
145	Titleist Acushnet 4	Cadwell Geer DT 100	1948	1	336 A	W	B
23	Titleist 6	Acushnet DT Red	1955	1	336 A	W	B
48	Titleist 6	Acushnet DT	1960	1	336 A	W	B
34	Acushnet 3	Club Special 3	1979	1	336 A	W	B

Figure 17.1 Vintage Titleist ATTI Dimple Pattern Golf Balls (336 A)

notebook number	pole label	seam label	date	chpt.	dimple pattern	BALL	CENTER	COVER
1	Titleist 4	Acushnet	1973	2	324 IA	W	LC	B
146	Titleist 2	Acushnet DT	1974	2	324 IA	W	LC	B
2	Titleist 7	Acushnet-Pro Traj	1975	2	324 IA	W	LC	B
4	Titleist 7	Pro Trajectory 100	1979	2	324 IA	W	LC	B
58	Titleist 3	Pro Trajectory 90	1979	2	324 IA	W	LC	B
13	PINNACLE 5		1982	2	324 IA	2P	SC	B
99	PINNACLE 1	PINNACLE 90	1987	2	332 IA	2P	SC	B
33	Pinnacle 4	332	1995	2	332 IA	2P	SC	S
31	384 PINNACLE 2	90 Compression	1987	2	384 IB	2P	SC	B
100	384 Pinnacle 2	90 COMPRESSION	1987	2	384 IB	2P	SC	B
116	Pinnacle 4	392 LS	1999	2	392 IB	2P	SC	S

Figure 17.2 Original Icosahedron Golf Balls (324 IA, 332 IA, 384 IB and 392 IB)

These Titleist golf balls were wound (W), had a liquid center (LC), and a balata cover (B). The Pinnacle golf balls were two-piece balls. One Pinnacle ball (#100) had a bright yellow cover. These golf balls are discussed in more detail in Chapter 2. The original icosahedron dimple pattern revolutionized the golf ball industry by providing increased distance compared to the golf balls with the ATTI dimple pattern.

Figure 17.3 shows the changes that have taken place for the DT Titleist golf ball over the period 1974 to 1985. These golf balls were called Durable Titleist because they had a Surlyn cover, which was very durable.

notebook number	pole label	seam label	date	chpt.	dimple pattern	BALL	CENTER	COVER
7	DT Titleist 8	Durable Titleist 90	1974	2	324 IA	W	LC	S
130	DT Titleist 5	Durable Titleist 90	1974	2	324 IA	W	LC	S
129	DT Titleist 4	Durable SURLYN	1976	2	324 IA	W	LC	S
6	DT Titleist 1	* 384 DT 90 *	1985	2	384 IB	W	LC	S
136	DT Titleist 3	* 384 DT 90 *	1985	2	384 IB	W	LC	S
138	DT Titleist 2	* 384 DT 90 *	1985	2	384 IB	W	LC	S

Figure 17.3 Durable Titleist Golf Balls

The original Durable Titleist golf balls were all wound balls with a liquid center. They were called Durable Titleist because they had a Surlyn cover (S), an ionomeric polymer that was very hard and durable. The original Surlyn covers did not cut or crack very easily when the golf ball wasn't struck correctly or when the ball hit a tree or the cart path. This was an improvement to the balata cover, which was easily damaged. For that reason recreational golfers preferred a golf ball with a

Surlyn cover. The first Durable Titleist golf balls had 324 dimples. But Titleist soon discovered that golf balls with 384 dimples, a hard cover, and a larger core traveled farther than golf balls with 324 dimples. Golf ball #136 had a bright yellow cover and #138 had an orange cover.

Figure 17.4 shows the changes that have taken place for the Titleist HVC, HP, HP2, and HP3 golf balls. The Titleist HVC golf ball is known for the fact that in 1992, it was the first Titleist model that had the solid two-piece construction rather than the wound construction.

notebook number	pole label	seam label	date	chpt.	dimple pattern	BALL	CENTER	COVER	SPIN
37	Titleist 4	* HVC 100 *	1992	4	440 CO	2P	SC	S	
153	Titleist 4	* HVC 90 *	1992	4	440 CO	2P	SC	S	
189	Ttileist 2	HVC Δ 90	1992	4	440 CO	2P	SC	S	
51	Titleist 3	HP2 Δ 100	1994	4	440 CO	2P	SC	1c	
84	Titleist 2	HP2 Δ 90	1994	4	440 CO	2P	SC	1c	
167	Titleist 4	HP2 Distance	1998	4	440 CO	2P	SC	1c	L-L
82	Titleist 1	HP2 Δ Distance	1998	4	440 CO	2P	SC	S	L-L
35	Titleist 3	HP2 Δ Tour	1998	4	440 CO	2P	SC	1c	L-M
166	Titleist 4	HP2 TOUR	1998	4	440 CO	2P	SC	1c	L-M
80	Titleist 1	< HP Tour >	2000	4	416 OQ	2P	SC	1c	L-M
141	Titleist 2	< HP >	2000	4	416 OQ	2P	SC	1c	L-M
54	Titleist 4	< HP ○ Distance >	2001	4	416 OQ	2P	SC	1c	L-M
36	Titleist 4	HVC Tour	2002	4	440 CO	2P	SC	1c	L-M
81	Titleist 2	HVC Soft Feel	2004	4	416 OQ	2P	SC	1c	L-M
140	Titleist 3	HVC – Soft Feel	2005	5	392 ID	2P	SC	1c	L-M
87	Titleist 2	<— HP3 Control —>	2007	5	392 ID	2P	SC	1c	L-M

Figure 17.4 HVC, HP, HP2 and HP3 Golf Balls

The HVC, HP, HP2 and HP3 golf balls are all two-piece golf balls with a solid center (SC) and a single cover (1c) made of Surlyn. There were three different types of dimple patterns for this category of golf balls. The 440 CO dimple pattern was a cuboctahedral pattern, and the 416 OQ dimple pattern was a regular octahedral pattern where each triangular region was constructed from three equivalent quadrilaterals. These are discussed in more detail in Chapter 4. The third dimple pattern was an icosahedron dimple pattern with 392 dimples in multiple sizes (392 ID). This pattern is discussed in Chapter 5. The spin rating (first introduced in the USGA conforming list at the end of the 1990s) for this category of golf ball was low spin with the driver and low spin with the lofted iron (L-L). Later the spin rating changed to L-M. This was probably due to the fact that the later models such as the Titleist HP2 switched to a ball with a soft Hytrel inner mantle layer and a Li Surlyn cover.[5]

Synopsis for Chapter Seventeen

- Vintage Titleist golf balls were all wound balls with liquid centers and soft balata covers.
- Vintage Pinnacle golf balls had solid cores and durable Surlyn covers.
- The Vintage DT Titleist golf ball were know as 'Durable Titleist' golf balls because they were the first Titleist golf balls with a Surlyn cover.
- The Titleist HVC, HP2, HP, and HP3 golf balls were all two piece balls with a solid core and a single cover.

Chapter Eighteen
Summary and Conclusions

A U.S. patent is a right granted to the inventor for a process, machine, product, or composition of matter that is new, useful, and not obvious. The patent gives the inventor an exclusive right to the technology for a limited time and prevents anyone else from making, using or selling the invention for a limited time. U.S. patents are also important teaching documents for those who take the time and effort to read and understand them. A patent is required to disclose everything about the invention so a person skilled in the art can understand and practice the invention once the patent term expires. In this chapter, I will summarize what I have learned about golf ball technology from my reading of the Acushnet Company patent literature. Also, I will summarize what I have learned about the golf ball dimple patterns, the USGA spin ratings, and the construction of the core and cover of Titleist and Pinnacle golf balls so that you can better understand the choices that are available to you when deciding among the various golf ball models that are available.

Long Distance Flight

Long distance flight results when you increase the size of the golf ball core and make the cover harder. This was discussed in Chapter 2, which disclosed a wound golf ball with a larger 1 1/8 inch core and a hard cover traveled farther than a wound golf ball with a smaller 1 1/16 inch core and a soft cover.

Longer distance results if the golf ball is a two-piece ball instead of a wound ball with a liquid center. The reason for this is because the resiliency (CoR) of a two-piece ball is higher than the resiliency of a wound ball with a liquid center. For a given swing speed, a two-piece ball has a higher initial velocity than a wound ball with a liquid center, resulting in longer distance.

Longer distance results if the golf ball dimple pattern has higher percent surface coverage. High percent surface coverage causes the air flow over the surface of the ball to become turbulent which reduces the area of the wake, which is the turbulent flow area behind the ball with low pressure. If the wake is reduced then the pressure behind the ball is increased and drag is reduced. This is true only if the dimples are of a reasonable size.

Longer distance results when the dimple pattern contains dimples of multiple sizes. This results in more efficient dimple packing and higher percent dimple surface coverage.

Longer distance results when no three dimples in a row have edges that are aligned on the surface of the golf ball. This gives the golf ball a high lift to drag ratio. This was discussed in Chapter 4.

Longer distance can result if the aerodynamics are optimized so that the golf ball has a relatively low lift coefficient (C_L) during ascent (high speed) and the ball travels further and may have more roll. Then during descent (low speed), a relatively high C_L is desirable to maximize the carry distance. This effect was optimized for high swing speed players by using high dimple volume golf balls with the 332 IE dimple pattern (Chapter 6)

Soft Golf Ball

A golf ball can be made to feel softer by making a softer core. This can be done in several ways. One way is to use CaO instead of ZnO as filler material in the core. Another way is to make a core using a high trans-PBD content, which results in a core with high resiliency (CoR) that is soft (low compression).

Another way to make a golf ball feel soft is to have a soft cover. An ionomer cover is a hard material and a cover made from an ionomer is hard. Creating a golf ball with a hard inner cover surrounded by a thin, soft outer cover produces a golf ball that feels soft. Soft cover materials are balata, polyurethane, and polyurea. You can make a hard ionomer cover softer by adding a softening co-monomer such as Hytrel® or other softening polymer. Another way to make a soft cover is by making a cover out of a highly neutralized ionomer polymer (HNP).

Spin

A golf ball that has a soft core and a soft cover will have high spin. A golf ball with a hard cover will have low spin.

A golf ball with high spin can be produced by having a multiple layer golf ball with a dense (high specific gravity) inner core and low specific gravity outer core and a soft cover. This construction results in a ball with a low moment of inertia (MOI) and high spin. A golf ball with low spin can be made by having a multiple layer golf ball with a low specific gravity inner core and a dense outer core and a hard cover. This construction results in a ball with a high moment of inertia and low spin.

Trajectory

A golf ball that has low dimple volume (shallow dimples) will have a high lift coefficient and will result in a golf ball that has high spin and a high trajectory. A golf ball that has a high dimple volume (deep dimples) will have a low lift coefficient and will result in a golf ball that has low spin and a low trajectory. Dimple volume can be adjusted by changing the edge angle of the dimples or if the dimples have a catenary curve dimple profile, by using a lower shape factor.

The dimple diameters on a golf ball with few dimples (the 252 I or 332 IE dimple patterns for example) will be larger than the dimple diameters on a golf ball with many dimples (392 ID or 440 CO dimple pattern). Larger dimples create more turbulence on the surface of the golf ball than small dimples. For a golfer with a high swing speed, lower dimple count can generate a shallower angle of descent resulting in a longer roll and longer total distance.

Feel

Two-piece balls were first constructed with a PBD core that had high cis-content and low trans-content. The PBD core on these balls was harder at the surface of the core and softer at the center of the core. This was called a large positive hardness gradient (the measured hardness at the surface minus the measured hardness at the center). These golf balls had high compression and felt hard. Golf balls that had higher amounts of trans-PBD in the core by varying the chemistry of core formation had softer feel. These golf balls had a low hardness gradient or a zero hardness gradient. A soft cover will make a golf ball feel softer overall.

Symmetric Flight

The early icosahedron dimple patterns, such as 392 IC, 392 ID, and 332 IE, were not spherically symmetrical. Part of the reason for this is because of the asymmetry caused by the parting line at the seam of the golf ball. This parting line can be eliminated by using seamless golf ball design discussed in Chapter 9.

Other parting lines occur on golf balls as a result of the dimple pattern that is chosen for the golf ball. These parting lines can be eliminated by choosing dimple pattern designs that don't have any parting lines. Tessellated dimple pattern designs discussed in Chapter 7 have high symmetry and few parting lines.

Symmetric flight can be improved on a golf ball by modifying some of the dimples in the polar region and/or in the equatorial region of the golf ball. The position of the dimples and how the dimples must be modified need to be determined using ballistic light screen technology.

Some golf ball dimple patterns that have multiple parting lines are, nonetheless, spherically symmetrical. The cuboctahedron dimple pattern is one example of a spherically symmetrical dimple pattern.

Slow Swing Speeds

Longer distance results for a golfer with a low or medium swing speed if the golf ball has low spin (high moment of inertia), high lift coefficient (shallow dimples), low drag coefficient, low core compression, and a hard cover. This ball produces a high trajectory and low spin rate.

For a golfer with a low swing speed, longer distance results if the golf ball has high spin (low moment of inertia), low lift coefficient (deep dimples), low drag coefficient, core compression greater than 70, and a soft cover. This ball produces a low trajectory and high spin rate.

Reduced Distance for Golfers with High Swing Speed

Reduced distance for golf balls struck by golfers with high swing speeds is needed so the USGA distance rule is not violated. Reduced distance, while maintaining a high performance trajectory, is possible by using a golf ball with the following: low CoR, reduced weight, increased size, low percent surface coverage, small dimples or dimples with increased edge angle or high dimple volume (resulting in low trajectory), increased C_D, and increased C_L.

Golf Ball Decision Criteria

This section is designed to help golfers choose the most appropriate 2017-2018 Titleist or Pinnacle golf ball based on a set of decision criteria. My decision criteria take into account only the following factors: the player's swing speed, the golf ball's spin ratio, the cost, and the color. Since 2011, all USGA conforming golf balls must meet the USGA symmetry standard and must meet the USGA distance standard. Therefore, golf ball symmetry and distance the ball will travel are not part of my decision criteria. For help to decide which older Titleist or Pinnacle golf ball models to choose, simply find the golf ball in the appropriate table in Chapters 11-17 and use the same information to rate the older golf balls as I used to rate the 2017-2018 models. Likewise, for golf balls that were made by companies other than Acushnet Company simply look in the USGA conforming golf ball list and/or the manufacturer's website to find the data that you may need.

To help you choose the most appropriate golf ball based on my decision criteria, first, determine your swing speed. A couple of ways to do this are discussed in Chapter 9. For our purposes, a low swing speed is less than about 70 mph, a medium swing speed is about 70-95 mph, and a high swing speed is greater than about 120 mph. Figure 18.1 shows the relationship of swing speed and carry distance for low, medium, and high swing speed players.

Golf Ball Cover Story

swing speed type	speed, mph	distance, yards
low	< 70	< 160
medium	70-95	160-219
high	120-130	276-300

Figure 18.1 Swing speed, distance for golfers with low, medium, and high swing speeds[1]

Next, if you are a golfer who cannot control unintentional side spin (slice or hook) when using your driver, you should probably consider only the golf balls with the L-L spin rating. If you have moderate control over unintentional side spin, then golf balls with the L-L and the L-M spin rating can be considered. Finally, if you have excellent control over unintentional side spin, golf balls with M-H spin rating can be used. For those of us on a budget, the cost[2] of golf balls can be a factor to consider also. For those of us who may be more fashion conscious, then the color[2] of the golf ball becomes important.

Table 18.2 shows the decision criteria that I have developed to help golfers choose which golf ball to use. Start by choosing the appropriate swing speed in column one, then choose the spin ratio that fits your ability in column two, then the MSRP in column three, and the golf ball color in column four. The golf ball that may be the best for you can be found in columns five and six based on my decision criteria. A golf ball with a pink color or a white golf ball with pink play number and seam label is assumed to be a golf ball with lower compression.

Golfer's Swing Speed	USGA Spin Ratio	MSRP, $/dozen	Ball Colors	Pole label	Seam label
low	L-L	$20	white[a]	Pinnacle	Soft
low	L-L	$20	pink	Pinnacle	Soft
low, medium	L-L	$20	white	Pinnacle	Soft
medium, high	L-L	$20	white, yellow	Pinnacle	Rush
low, medium	L-L	$29	pink	Titleist	Velocity
medium, high	L-L	$29	white, orange	Titleist	Velocity
low, medium	L-M	$24	white, yellow	Titleist	DT Trusoft
medium	L-M	$38	white, yellow	Titleist	Tour Soft
medium	L-M	$52	white, yellow	Titleist	AVX
low, medium	M-H	$52	white[a]	Titleist	Pro V1
medium, high	M-H	$52	white	Titleist	Pro V1
high	M-H	$52	white	Titleist	Pro V1x

[a] white with pink play number and seam label

Table 18.2 Decision criteria for golf ball choices

The Pinnacle Soft golf ball is a two-piece ball with an L-L spin rating. It is a good choice for a golfer who cannot control unintentional side spin (hook and slice). It costs $20/dozen and the golf balls come in white, pink, and white with pink number and seam label. The white ball may have higher compression (for a faster swing speed player) than either the pink ball or the white ball with pink number and seam label (for a lower swing speed player). These balls may perform well for golfers with either a low or medium swing speed. They have a soft core and a soft cover and they feel softer than the Pinnacle Rush.

The Pinnacle Rush golf ball is a two-piece ball with an L-L spin rating. It costs $20/dozen and it comes in white and optic yellow. This ball has a relatively hard core and a soft ionomer cover. This ball may perform well for golfers with a medium and a high swing speed. It has a hard feel compared to the Pinnacle Soft.

The Titleist Velocity is a two-piece ball with an L-L spin rating. It costs $29/dozen and comes in white, orange, and pink. It has very fast initial velocity of any Titleist golf ball and it has a high flight trajectory and may perform well for golfers of all swing speeds depending on the compression.

The Titleist DT Trusoft is a two-piece ball with an L-M spin rating. This ball will have low spin off the driver and higher spin with a lofted iron shot to the green. This ball costs $24/dozen and is available in white and optic yellow. It may perform well for golfers with low to medium swing speed.

The Titleist TOUR SOFT golf ball is a two-piece ball with an L-M spin rating. This balls costs $38/dozen and is available in white and optic yellow. This golf ball was introduced in 2018 and it replaced the Titleist NXT Tour golf ball. The soft core and soft cover provide good distance and good feel. This ball may perform well for golfers with a medium swing speed.

The Titleist AVX was introduced in 2018 to replace the Titleist NXT Tour golf ball. Availability is limited to a test market in participating golf shops in California, Arizona, and Florida. This ball is a three-piece ball that has an inner core, an outer core and a soft cover. The spin rating is L-M and this ball may perform well for golfers with a medium swing speed. The cost for the Titleist AVX is $52/dozen.

The Titleist Pro V1 golf ball is a three-piece ball with a solid core, an intermediate casing layer, and a urethane cover. This ball has a spin rating of M-H which means it has medium spin with the driver and high spin with a lofted iron. This ball costs $52/dozen and it was designed for the golfer who can control the golf ball spin with the driver and who wants to create backspin with a lofted club to stop the ball quickly on the green. This ball may perform well for golfers of all swing speeds. The ball comes in white with a black number and seam label and in white with a pink number and seam label (lower compression).

The Titleist Pro V1x is a four-piece ball with a solid center, a solid outer core, an intermediate casing layer, and a urethane cover. This ball may perform well for a golfer who is able to control unintentional side spin and who has a high swing speed. This ball costs $52/dozen and it comes only in white.

Well, I hope you have found this information useful and helpful in making golf ball choices. Many golf pro shops have used golf balls for sale—those that were found on the course and cleaned up for resale. This may be an inexpensive way for golfers to try out a new golf ball to see if they like it. Of course, don't expect that choosing a different golf ball using my decision criteria will solve all your golfing woes. A golf ball can only do so much to help improve your golf scores and increase your enjoyment of the game. A better option to improve your golf game may be to see a PGA professional for swing lessons. Plus, don't forget to practice.

Synopsis Chapter Eighteen

- This chapter summarizes all the golf ball technology that I have learned from reading the patent literature from Acushnet Company.
- This chapter introduces a set of decision criteria to help golfers choose the best golf ball they should use based on their swing speed, their ability to control unintentional side spin, their budget, and their preferences.

Glossary

Aerodynamics : The study of the interaction of air with a solid object.

Antioxidant: A molecule that inhibits the oxidation of another molecule.

Balata: A hard rubber-like material from the sap of a tropical tree. It is a polymer of isoprene.

Another name for balata is gutta-percha.

Castable: A plastic object capable of being cast in a mold.

Coefficient of restitution (CoR): The ratio of the initial to final velocity of two objects after they collide. A coefficient of restitution of 1.0 is a perfectly elastic collision and a coefficient of restitution of 0.0 is inelastic.

Compression: A measure of the softness/hardness of a golf ball. In the 1920's Raphael Atti built the first golf ball compression tester to compare golf balls. A ball with a high compression has a higher velocity off the club face than a ball with a low compression.

Elastic modulus: A number that measures an object's resistance to being deformed elastically when a stress is applied to that object.

Flexural modulus: A number that measures an object's resistance to being deformed when a bending force is applied to that object.

High modulus: A material that has a high modulus is a stiff material that only slightly changes its shape when deformed.

Low modulus: A material that has a low modulus is a flexible material that changes its shape easily when deformed.

Moment of inertia: A measure of how difficult it will be to rotate an object when a force is applied to it. An object with a high moment of inertia means it is difficult to rotate.

Orthographic projection: A means of representing three-dimentional objects in two dimensions.

Quadrilateral: A four sided shape with straight sides.

Specific gravity: The ratio of the density of a substance relative to that of water. If the specific gravity is 1.0, then the object is denser than water.

Tessellate: To arrange in a checkered or mosaic pattern.

Thermoset: A material that hardens permanently after one application of heat and pressure.

Thermoplastic: A material that becomes soft when heated and hard when cooled.

Vulcanization: A chemical process that makes rubber more durable by heating it with a sulfur compound that cross-links the individual polymer chains.

ENDNOTES

Introduction

1. John F. Hotchkiss, *500 Years of Golf Balls: History & Collector's Guide* (Iowa: Antique Trader Books, 1997). This book contains a reprint of John Stuart Martin, *The Curious History of the Golf Ball, Mankind's Most Fascinating Sphere*, (New York: Horizon Press, 1968).
2. Frank S. Martin, Thaddeus A. Pietraszek, and Peter Dornik, Jr., US 2,728,576, Dec. 27, 1955, priority date Dec. 10, 1953.
3. Photo by Albert Harrison, press photographer Meriden Record Journal, summer 1963.

Chapter One

1. John F. Hotchkiss, *500 Years of Golf Balls: History & Collector's Guide* (Iowa: Antique Trader Books, 1997). This book contains a reprint of John Stuart Martin, *The Curious History of the Golf Ball, Mankind's Most Fascinating Sphere*, (New York: Horizon Press, 1968), pg 119.
2. William Taylor, US 878,254, Feb. 4, 1908, filed Sep. 11, 1906.
3. Reference 1, pg 126.
4. Bertram G. Work, Coburn Haskell, US 622,834, Apr. 11, 1899, filed Aug. 9, 1898.
5. John R. Gammeter, US 647,256, Apr 10, 1900, filed Dec 20, 1899.
6. Kurt E. Wilhelm, US 2,425,909, Aug 19, 1947, filed Dec 14, 1945. See also Melvin Mooney US 2,493,259, Jan 3, 1950, filed July 18, 1946.
7. Frank H. Mingay, US 889,709, June 2, 1908, filed Apr. 7, 1906.
8. W.C. Geer, *The Reign of Rubber* (New York: The Century Co, 1922), pg 100, http://books.google.com.
9. William C. Geer, US 1,524,428, Jan. 27, 1925, filed Apr. 19, 1921.
10. Reference 8, pg 272.
11. Sidney M. Cadwell, US 1.951,392, Mar. 20, 1934, filed Sep. 2, 1931.
12. Glenn D. Babcock, *History of the United States Rubber Company: A Case Study in Corporation Management* (Indiana Business Report No. 39, Bureau of Business Research, Graduate School of Business, Indiana University, Indiana University, 1966), pg 345.
13. Udo Machat and Larry Dennis, *The Golf Ball Book*, (Sport Images, 7211 Woodrow Drive. Oakland, California 94611, USA, 2000), p 83.
14. http://www.titleist.com/company/titleist-story
15. These numbers refer to the pages in my golf ball notebook.
16. M. Hatcher, *The History of Titleist (Acushnet) Golf Balls (Science Resort (SR) LLC*, 2014, pg 7.

17. Reference 16, pg 10.
18. Kurt E. Wilhelm, US 2,425,909, Aug. 19, 1947, filed Dec. 14, 1945.
19. Reference 16, pg 13.
20. Reference 16, pg 16.

Chapter Two

1. https://en.wikipedia.org/wiki/Regular_octahedron
2. https://en.wikipedia.org/wiki/Regular_icosahedron
3. Frank deS. Lynch, John W. Jepson, Robert A. Brown, GB 1,381,897, Jan. 29, 1975, filed Mar 20, 1972.
4. Frank deS. Lynch, John W. Jepson, Robert A. Brown, US 4,729,861, Mar. 8, 1988 priority date Mar 20, 1972.
5. Frank deS. Lynch, John W. Jepson, Robert A. Brown, US 4,936,587, Jun. 26, 1990 priority date Mar 20, 1972.
6. Frank deS. Lynch, John W. Jepson, Robert A. Brown, US 5,080,367, Jan. 14, 1992 priority date Mar 20, 1972.
7. https://en.wikipedia.org/wiki/Platonic_solid
8. John F. Hotchkiss, *500 Years of Golf Balls: History & Collector's Guide* (Iowa: Antique Trader Books, 1997). This book contains a reprint of John Stuart Martin, *The Curious History of the Golf Ball, Mankind's Most Fascinating Sphere*, (New York: Horizon Press, 1968), pg 120.
9. http://www.funduniverse.com/company-histories/acushnet-company-history/
10. Francis deS. Lynch, John W. Jepson, Robert A. Brown, Des. 237,983, Dec. 9, 1975, filed Mar. 1973.
11. http://www.golfballtool.com/compressor_hist.htm
12. GB 1,364,138, 21 Aug 1974, filed 17 Jan 1972.
13. https://en.wikipedia.org/wiki/Thales'_theorem
14. William Gobush, Raymond A. Berard, Robert A. Brown, John W. Jepson, US 4,858,923, Aug 22, 1989 priority date Oct 24, 1983.
15. Philip E. Young, US 2,058,201, Oct 20, 1936, filed May 4, 1936.
16. Udo Machat and Larry Dennis, *The Golf Ball Book*, (Sport Images, 7211 Woodrow Drive. Oakland, California 94611, USA, 2000), p 121.
17. Richard Watkin Rees, US 3,264,272, Aug 2, 1966, filed Apr 8, 1963.
18. Robert P. Molitor, US 3,819,768, June 25, 1974, filed Feb 11, 1972.
19. Reference 9, pg 112.

Chapter Three

1. William Gobush, Raymond A. Berard, Robert A. Brown, John w. Jepson, US 4,915,390 Apr 10 1990, priority date Oct 24 1983.
2. William Gobush, US 4,804,189 Feb. 14, 1989, priority date Oct. 24, 1983.
3. William Gobush, US 4,949,976 Aug. 21, 1990, priority date Oct. 24, 1983.
4. William Gobush, US 4,960,283 Oct. 2, 1990, priority date Oct. 24, 1983.
5. William Gobush, US 5,060,954 Oct. 29, 1991, priority date Oct. 24, 1983.

6. Dates of production were obtained from a spreadsheet available for the period 1963-2002 that was obtained from Acushnet Co, 333 Bridge Street, Fairhaven Massachusetts, 1-800-225-8500.
7. Robert A. Brown, US 4,783,078 Nov. 8, 1988, filed Feb. 27, 1987.
8. Edmund A. Hebert, William E. Morgan, Dean Snell, US 5,885,172, Mar. 23, 1999, filed May 27, 1997.
9. John F. Hotchkiss, *500 Years of Golf Balls: History & Collector's Guide* (Iowa: Antique Trader Books, 1997). This book contains a reprint of John Stuart Martin, *The Curious History of the Golf Ball, Mankind's Most Fascinating Sphere*, (New York: Horizon Press, 1968), pg 120.

Chapter Four

1. Steven Aoyama, US 4,948,143, Aug 14, 1990, filed Jul. 6, 1989.
2. https://en.wikipedia.org/wiki/Cuboctahedron
3. The equation for calculating percent surface coverage is disclosed in US 4,804,189, Feb. 14, 1989, priority date Oct. 24, 1983.
4. Steven Aoyama, US 4,960,281, Oct. 2, 1990, filed Oct. 17, 1989.
5. Steven Aoyama US 5,957,786, Sep. 28, 1999, filed Sep. 3, 1997.
6. John F. Hotchkiss, *500 Years of Golf Balls: History & Collector's Guide* (Iowa: Antique Trader Books, 1997). This book contains a reprint of John Stuart Martin, *The Curious History of the Golf Ball, Mankind's Most Fascinating Sphere*, (New York: Horizon Press, 1968), pg 147.
7. George C. Schweiker, John W. Jepson, US 3,791,655, Feb. 12, 1974, filed Dec. 1, 1971.
8. Paul M. Gendreau, Francisco M. Llort, Raymond a. Berard, US 4,546,980, Oct. 15, 1985, filed Sep. 4, 1984.
9. Leonidas A. Keches, Sharon R. Goggin, Edward J. Issac, Ronald J. Rogers, US 4,323,247, Apr. 6, 1982, filed Jan. 19, 1981.
10. Sharon R. Issac, US 5,000,459, Mar. 19, 1991, filed Jul. 5, 1989.
11. Steven Aoyama, US 5,158,300, Oct. 27, 1992, filed Oct 24, 1991.
12. Steven Aoyama US 5,415,410, May 16, 1995, filed Feb. 7, 1994.
13. William E. Morgan and Steven Aoyama, US 6,849,007, Feb. 1, 2005, filed Feb. 11, 2003.

Chapter Five

1. Steven Aoyama, US 5,957,786, Sep. 28, 1999, filed Sep. 3, 1997.
2. Steven Aoyama, US 6,358,161, Mar. 19, 2002, filed Sep. 27, 1999.
3. The equation for calculating percent surface coverage is disclosed in US 4,804,189, Feb. 14, 1989, priority date Oct. 24, 1983.
4. Laurent C. Bissonnette, Jeffrey L. Dalton, and Steven Aoyama, US 6,729,976, May 4, 2004, filed Mar. 14, 2003.
5. Laurent C. Bissonnette, Jeffrey L. Dalton, and Steven Aoyama, US 6,913,550, Jul, 5, 2005, filed Feb. 24, 2004.
6. Laurent C. Bissonnette, Jeffrey L. Dalton, and Steven Aoyama, US 7,156,757, Jan. 2, 2007, filed Apr. 19, 2005.
7. Laurent C. Bissonnette, Jeffrey L. Dalton, and Steven Aoyama, US 7,491,137, Feb. 17, 2009, filed Oct. 10, 2007.

8. Douglas Winfield and William Gobush, US 6,285,445, Sep. 4, 2001, filed Sep. 17, 1999.
9. The Aerodynamic Criteria depends on the size and weight of the golf ball.
10. This was calculated using the equation $\omega = (2*SR * V)/ D$; where the ω is the ball rotation, SR is the Spin Ratio, V is the ball velocity, and D is the ball diameter.
11. Steven Aoyama, Paul A. Puniello, Robert A. Wilson, US 7,422,529, Sep. 9, 2008, filed Mar. 10, 2004.
12. Steven Aoyama, US 5,158,300, Oct. 27, 1992, filed Oct. 24, 1991.
13. Frank deS. Lynch, John W. Jepson, Robert A. Brown, US 4,729,861, Mar 8, 1988 priority date Mar 20, 1972.
14. Jeffrey L. Dalton and Laurent Bissonnette, US 6,796,912, Sep. 28, 2004, filed Nov. 21, 2001.
15. Steven Aoyama, and Nicholas M. Nardacci, US 7,887,439, Feb. 15, 2011, filed Dec. 8, 2009.
16. M. Hatcher, *The History of Titleist (Acushnet) Golf Balls* (Science Resort (SR) LLC, 2014), pg 129.
17. Reference 16, pg 139.
18. This golf ball has a partially transparent cover and a pink intermediate layer that is disclosed in US 7,722,483.
19. Reference 16, pg 152.

Chapter Six

1. Steven Aoyama, Douglas E. Jones, US 6,916,255, Jul. 12, 2005, filed Jan. 6, 2003.
2. Steven Aoyama, Douglas E. Jones, US 6,923,736, Aug. 2, 2005, filed Jan. 6, 2003.
3. Steven Aoyama, Douglas E. Jones, US 6,945,880, Sep. 20, 2005, filed Jan. 6, 2003.
4. Steven Aoyama, Douglas E. Jones, US 7,033,287, Apr. 25, 2006, filed Oct. 13, 2004.
5. Steven Aoyama, Douglas E. Jones, US 7,226,369, Jun. 5, 2007, filed Dec. 14, 2005.
6. Steven Aoyama, Douglas E. Jones, US 7,473,195, Jan. 6, 2009, filed Mar. 7, 2007.
7. Christopher Cavallaro, Ryan B. Bosanko, Edmund A. Hebert, US 6,913,547, Jul. 5, 2005, filed Feb. 13, 2001.
8. Jeffrey L. Dalton, Kevin M. Harris, Laurent C. Bissonnette, Derek A. Ladd, Steven M. Gosetti, Samuel A. Pasqua, US 6,180,722, Jan. 30, 2001, filed Sep. 25, 1998.
9. This golf ball has a partially transparent cover and a pink intermediate layer that is disclosed in US 7,722,483.
10. Jeffrey L. Dalton and Laurent Bissonnette, US 6,796,912, Sep. 28, 2004, filed Nov. 21, 2001.

Chapter Seven

1. Steven Aoyama, Nicholas M. Nardacci, US Application 2010/0240473, Sep. 23, 2010, filed Mar. 20, 2009.
2. Nicholas M. Nardacci, Michael R. Madson, US 8,029,388, Oct. 4, 2011, filed Oct. 31, 2008.
3. Michael R. Madson, Nicholas M. Nardacci, US 9,440,115, Sep. 13, 2016, filed Mar. 14, 2011.
4. Michael R. Madson, Nicholas M. Nardacci, US 9,468,810, Oct. 18, 2016, filed Aug. 22, 2013.

5. Steven Aoyama, Paul A. Puniello, Robert A. Wilson, US 7,422,529, Sep. 9, 2008, filed Mar. 10, 2004.
6. Nicholas M. Nardacci, Steven Aoyama, Robert A. Wilson, US 7,431,670, Oct. 7, 2008, filed Sep. 17, 2007.
7. Nicholas M. Nardacci, Steven Aoyama, Robert A. Wilson, US 7,618,333, Nov. 17, 2009, filed Sep. 25, 2008.
8. Michael R. Madson, Nicholas M. Nardacci, David P. Hunt, US 9,174,088, Nov. 3, 2015, filed Sep. 24, 2012.
9. https://en.wikipedia.org/wiki/Tetrahedron
10. Michael R. Madson, Nicholas M. Nardacci, US D627,838 S, Nov. 23, 2010, filed May 20, 2010.
11. Michael R. Madson, Nicholas M. Nardacci, US D627,016 S, Nov. 9, 2010, filed May 20, 2010.
12. Michael R. Madson, Nicholas M. Nardacci, US D627,017 S, Nov. 9, 2010, filed May 20, 2010.
13. Michael R. Madson, Nicholas M. Nardacci, US 2016/0375310 A1, Dec. 29, 2016, filed Sep. 12, 2016.
14. Michael R. Madson, Nicholas M. Nardacci, Steven Aoyama, US 8,632,425, Jan. 21, 2014, filed Sep. 20, 2010.
15. Michael R. Madson, Nicholas M. Nardacci, US 9,782,628, Oct. 10, 2017, filed Jan. 21, 2014.

Chapter Eight

1. The USGA rules can be found on the USGA website at www.usga.org
2. "USGA letter to manufacturer takes ball debate to new level," by D. Seanor, Golfweek, pp. 4, 26, Apr. 23, 2005.
3. Michael J. Sullivan, Steven Aoyama, Edmund A. Hebert, Derek A. Ladd, William E. Morgan, and Michael D. Jordan, US 7,481,723, Jan. 27, 2009, filed Aug. 29, 2005.
4. Michael J. Sullivan, Steven Aoyama, Edmund A. Hebert, Derek A. Ladd, William E. Morgan, and Michael D. Jordan, US 7,909,711, Mar. 22, 2011, filed Jan. 12, 2009.
5. Michael J. Sullivan and Steven Aoyama, US 7,938,745, May 10, 2011, filed Dec. 10, 2008.
6. Michael J. Sullivan and Steven Aoyama, US 8,152,656, Apr. 10, 2012, filed Apr. 7, 2011.
7. https://www.titleist.com

Chapter Nine

1. William E. Morgan, Herbert C. Boehm, Steven Aoyama, US 6,299,552, Oct. 9, 2001, filed Apr. 20, 1999.
2. Michael J. Sullivan, Derek A. Ladd, Edmund A. Hebert, Laurent Bissonnette, US 8,617,003, Dec. 31, 2014, filed Jan. 18, 2006.
3. Michael J. Sullivan, Derek A. Ladd, Edmund A. Hebert, Laurent Bissonnette, US 8,956,249, Feb. 17, 2015, filed Jul. 11, 2013.
4. Michael J. Sullivan, Derek A. Ladd, Edmund A. Hebert, Laurent Bissonnette, US 9,440,119, Sep. 13, 2016, filed Nov. 12, 2014.

Chapter Ten

1. https://en.wikipedia.org/wiki/Term_of_patent_in_the_United_States
2. John F. Hotchkiss, *500 Years of Golf Balls: History & Collector's Guide* (Iowa: Antique Trader Books, 1997). This book contains a reprint of John Stuart Martin, *The Curious History of the Golf Ball, Mankind's Most Fascinating Sphere*, (New York: Horizon Press, 1968), pg. 120.
3. https://www.usga.org/ConformingGolfBall/gball_list.pdf
4. This was done by painstaking searching on the web. Copies of these lists can be found on my website: https://golfballcoverstory.com

Chapter Eleven

1. Edmund A. Hebert, William E. Morgan, Dean Snell, US 5,885,172, Mar. 23, 1999, filed May 27, 1997.
2. Edmund A. Hebert, William E. Morgan, Dean Snell, US 6,132,324, Oct. 17, 2000, filed Dec. 9, 1998.
3. http://golf-patents.com/an-update-on-the-latest-golf-ball-patent-infrin...
4. http://www.sandiegouniontribune.com/business/technology/sdut-calla...
5. http://blog.lostgolfballs.com/pro-v1-vs-pro-v1x-the-truth-revealed
6. https://www.usga.org/ConformingGolfBall/gball_list.pdf
7. I thank my friend Tim Wallace, the jeweler, for letting me use his chemical balance to weigh the golf balls.
8. https://www.titleist.com/company/patents
9. Shenshen Wu, Edmund A. Hebert, Laurent Bissonnette, David A. Bulpett, Murali Rajagopalan, Peter Voorheis, mark N. Wrigley, US 6,486,261, Nov. 26, 2002, filed Nov. 27, 2000.
10. Brian Comeau, Michael J. Sullivan, Douglas E. Jones, Derek A. Ladd, US 8,845,456, Sep. 30, 2014, filed Dec. 21, 2012.

Chapter Twelve

1. Michael D. Jordan, Jeffrey L. Dalton, Christopher Cavallaro, US 6,634,964, oct. 21, 2003, filed Feb. 13, 2002.
2. I am assuming that the seam label for the Pro V1x golf ball follows the same naming pattern as the seam label for the Pro V1 golf ball reported in the reference: http://blog.lostgolfballs.com/pro-v1-vs-pro-v1x-the-truth-revealed
3. https://www.usga.org/ConformingGolfBall/gball_list.pdf
4. I thank my friend Tim Wallace, the jeweler, for letting me use his chemical balance to weigh the golf balls.
5. https://www.livestrong.com/article/350627-golf-clubs-80-mph-swing-speed/
6. Edmund A. Hebert, Christopher Cavallaro, US 7,335,114, Feb. 26, 2008, filed Oct. 28, 20015.
7. David A. Bulpett, Brian Comeau, Derek A. Ladd, Michael J. Sullivan, US 7,537,530, May 26, 2009, filed Jul. 27, 2007.
8. David A. Bulpett, Brian Comeau, Derek A. Ladd, Michael J. Sullivan, US 9,636,549, May 2, 2017, filed Apr. 21, 2015.
9. Michael J. Sullivan, Brian Comeau, Dennis Britton, US 9,669,267, Jun. 6, 2017, filed Jul. 8, 2015.

Chapter Thirteen

1. Derek A. Ladd, Laurent Bissonnette, David A. Bulpett, Mark N. Wrigley, US 6,417,278, Jul. 9, 2002, filed May 22, 2000.
2. Previous attempts to reduce the compression of a cis-polybutadiene core resulted in an undesirable reduction in the resiliency also.
3. Walter L. Reid, Jr., Stephen K. Scolamiero, Thomas E. Moore, John W. Kennedy, Steven Earle, Daniel Ditzel, US 6,645,414, Nov. 11, 2003, filed Oct. 11, 2001.
4. Christopher Cavallaro, Jeffrey L. Dalton, Michael D. Jordan, Herbert C. Boehm, Samuel A. Pasqua, Jr., US 6,517,451, Feb. 11, 2003, filed Mar. 8, 2001.

Chapter Sixteen

1. M. Hatcher, *The History of Titleist (Acushnet) Golf Balls (Science Resort (SR) LLC, 2014, pg 125.*
2. Reference 1, pg 129.
3. Reference 1, pg 139.
4. Reference 1, pg 152.

Chapter Seventeen

1. John F. Hotchkiss, *500 Years of Golf Balls: History & Collector's Guide* (Iowa: Antique Trader Books, 1997). This book contains a reprint of John Stuart Martin, *The Curious History of the Golf Ball, Mankind's Most Fascinating Sphere*, (New York: Horizon Press, 1968).
2. Udo Machat and Larry Dennis, *The Golf Ball Book,* (Sport Images, 7211 Woodrow Drive. Oakland, California 94611, USA, 2000).
3. M. Hatcher, *The History of Titleist (Acushnet) Golf Balls (Science Resort (SR) LLC,* 2014.
4. See Chapter 10 for additional discussion.
5. Reference 2, pg 147.

Chapter Eighteen

1. http://www.swingmangolf.com/average-golf-swing-speed-chart-2/
2. https://www.titleist.com/account

ACKNOWLEDGEMENTS

I would like to thank my wife Laura for her encouragement and understanding during the writing of this book. She has supported me in every aspect of this project for which I am extremely grateful. Special thanks also for her photo of the golf course that appears on the back cover. I would also like to thank my son Dan for his help and expertise in designing the artwork for the cover of this book. His talent and abilities are greatly appreciated. His artwork can be viewed on his website http://www.hjmooijink.com/. Special thanks also to my son Eli for his help in proofreading the manuscript and for answering numerous questions about format and general information about grammar and punctuation. For those who are also interested in his music, please visit his website at https://eliharrison.com/.

I owe a very special thank you to my good friend Edmond Addeo, an acclaimed author, who encouraged me to write this book and who also was able to connect me with Waterfront Press. I want to thank my friend and former work associate Claude Caroli, with whom I have been able to consult and commiserate. Thanks also to my good friend Patty Friesen for help in reviewing the manuscript and for helpful suggestions. Thank you to my good friend Terry Friesen for his helpful discussion on the science of aerodynamics. Special thanks also go to Dr. Nancy Derham and her staff, Dana Allen, Raz Bomar, and Chris Mattos, for their help in obtaining the x-ray photos of the golf balls. Thanks also to my friend and fellow Spanish student Tim Wallace for letting me use his jewelry balance to measure the weight of many of the golf balls in my collection.

Thank you also to my golfing buddies who either donated golf balls to my golf ball collection, or put up with me when I wouldn't stop talking about this project: Ted Bakkila, Dick Lasus, Tri Tran, Gary Spitzack, Rich Lee, Stan Lauchner (apologies for not including your golf ball weighing puzzle in my book), Curt Campbell, Wilt Biggs, and especially Pete Stonebraker, who provided valuable encouragement and support to me after reading early drafts of the manuscript.

www.ingramcontent.com/pod-product-compliance
Lightning Source LLC
Chambersburg PA
CBHW041521220426
43669CB00002B/16